T0243239

Abuela's
Plant-Based Kitchen

Abuela's Plant-Based Kitchen

Vegan Cuisine Inspired by Latin & Caribbean Family Recipes

75 Multicultural Meals

 Karla Salinari, *certified holistic health coach*

Skyhorse Publishing

Skyhorse Publishing books may be purchased in bulk at special discounts for sales promotion, corporate gifts, fund-raising, or educational purposes. Special editions can also be created to specifications. For details, contact the Special Sales Department, Skyhorse Publishing, 307 West 36th Street, 11th Floor, New York, NY 10018 or info@skyhorsepublishing.com.

Skyhorse® and Skyhorse Publishing® are registered trademarks of Skyhorse Publishing, Inc.®, a Delaware corporation.

Visit our website at www.skyhorsepublishing.com.

10 9 8 7 6 5 4 3 2

Library of Congress Cataloging-in-Publication Data is available on file.

Cover design by David Ter-Avanesyan
Cover photography by Zuleika Acosta
Food styling by Sophia Loch
Art direction (photography, layout) by Faride Mereb

Print ISBN: 978-1-5107-7271-7
Ebook ISBN: 978-1-5107-7272-4

Printed in China

Dedicated to my daughter, Carolina. You inspire me every day.

Contents

Foreword

I found my way to plant-based eating after being diagnosed with cancer, twice. Since my recovery, I've been spreading the word about plant-based nutrition as a fundamental tool against fighting diseases. It has been my experience that plants have the power to unlock a healthier, more vibrant life and well-being. I'm so glad to see a shift in the world toward embracing this new way to care for ourselves. Karla's take on preserving the culinary traditions of Puerto Rico while incorporating new ingredients is a gift to our community. I hope you discover the power of plants and the secret to well-being through these amazing recipes.

—En vida y en salud,

Draco Rosa, Puerto Rican singer, musician, songwriter, and plant-based advocate

Introduction

"Lo hice con todo mi amor."

Lo hice con todo mi amor is what my mom used to say about the meals she cooked for me: *I made it with all my love.* My relationship with food has been a journey, but where the journey starts and ends is with love. So, before we go any further, let's go back to the very beginning.

Growing up, I lived in two culinary worlds: one in Miami and one in Puerto Rico. My parents divorced when I was young, so I split time between Miami (with my mom and my brother, Manny) and in Puerto Rico (with my dad and his family).

While living in Miami, food was my consistent connection to Caribbean culture. My mom cooked traditional Puerto Rican dishes like steaming, savory plates of *arroz con pollo.* I had a Cuban stepfather whose background influenced how my mom cooked, too. When I was in Puerto Rico with my dad, on the other hand, I ate differently. He was an early adopter of a plant-based diet, rich in whole foods and vegetables (with the occasional tofu nugget thrown in for me, of course). To me, food was always a signifier of all the places that I called home and of the cultural mash-up that made my family unique.

I spent a lot of time with my mom's parents, *Abuelo* and *Abuela*, and my dad's parents, *Abi* and *Mami Abuelita*. A lot of the recipes I grew up eating went back to my grandparents' generation. Mami Abuelita kept a composition notebook with recipes written in shorthand. When I started this project, I poured over her aged notebook with its yellowed pages, deciphering her notes and thinking about how I could translate her recipes for this book. I started to see the lineage of my family and where so many of the recipes I'd enjoyed growing up came from.

I believe that food is always intertwined with our families, our identities, and our memories. When I recall my childhood, I'm equally nostalgic when I think of making boxed scalloped potatoes with Manny in Miami and watching my abuela make her famous *avena* (oatmeal) on her stove top in Puerto Rico. I loved all the foods that made me who I was. When you're a kid, food is simple. You just enjoy it.

For example, when I was little, I loved these little canned sausages, which are super popular in Puerto Rico. I remember peeling the skin and eating them slowly to savor every bite! I didn't think twice about what I ate. I accepted it as a source of joy, comfort, and of course, fuel. It wasn't until much later that it all got more complicated.

When I was pregnant with my daughter, Carolina (we call her Caro), I gained eighty-two pounds. I remember being laser-focused on losing my postpartum weight, instead of stepping back and looking at my mindset around food. I tried countless fad diets and even diet pills. In addition to feeling like a nervous wreck from the pills, nothing ever stuck, and the weight stayed on. There was no way to integrate a restrictive diet into my everyday life because that meant losing out on the foods I loved. How could I commit to that long term?

After a while, I had completely lost my ability to connect with food in the way I always had: from a place of joy. I believe that a big reason why most diets don't work is because they take away our ability to enjoy the foods that nourish our soul and give us a sense of belonging. When I think about that time in my life, I think about how much deprivation and frustration I experienced and how it never gave me the results I wanted.

And so, on my maternity leave, alone and afraid that I was in for a lifetime of feeling unwell in my new postpartum body, I started my health journey. I examined my relationship with food, my roots, and how I could integrate the two culinary worlds I'd moved between. How could I get back to loving myself and food again? How could I reconnect with my body and give it what it needed? I required a totally different mindset. I had to approach my health with the love and care that my family had when they fed me.

Like most people trying to get healthier, I didn't know where to start. In order to get back to myself, I looked at where I came from. My dad had given me a glimpse into an alternative way of eating and my Aunt Tata and Uncle Soto even had a popular restaurant in Puerto Rico called Restaurante Vegetariano. Their restaurant was ahead of its time, serving up veggie-rich alternatives to classic dishes like *pastelón* and *arroz con gandules* in the eighties when vegetarianism was considered unpopular and most Puerto Rican dishes were made using lard, store-bought *Sazón* with additives and preservatives and meat bouillon cubes. Plant-based eating has never been strange to me, even if I'd never fully embraced it for myself. During the time that I was searching for a solution, going "plant-based" was gaining momentum. Maybe I could discover my path to health through eating more plants?

As I reflected, I remembered what I learned from my mom, aunts, and grandmothers, who were all fantastic, self-taught cooks. They had shown me that taking the time to make a meal for yourself and others was a simple, wholesome act of love. I have always admired their cooking and was regularly making many of their recipes, which had been passed down through the family. I wondered if maybe there was a way to make these dishes with less meat and more vitamins and minerals by way of plant-based ingredients.

Looking to my past gave me the courage to start a new beginning. I knew that if I did, it would have a positive ripple effect on my new daughter as she grew up. I wanted to set a good example. I began reading every book I could find on nutrition and plant-based eating. It was a scattershot attempt to educate myself in order to adopt a healthier lifestyle, but I wanted to do better, and I craved more information. I read about how overly processed foods can wreak havoc on our digestive systems and how eating less dairy can clear up skin problems. I learned that vitamin A is critical for good vision and which foods have disease-fighting antioxidants.

As Caro got older, we started baking, but I flipped some of the recipes into being plant-based with my new knowledge. I started experimenting by subbing out eggs for ripe bananas and using oat flour. This eventually became the foundation for my successful FlipBox Cake in a box, a healthier alternative to boxed cake mix that you can make with kids.

I was hooked on plant-based eating and flipping recipes—I couldn't stop! I wanted to learn more and encourage others with the same anxiety and fear I'd had around eating by flipping recipes into healthier ones, simply by upgrading a few favorite dishes. A friend who noticed my passion suggested I look into IIN, the International Institute of Nutrition, and I enrolled in a program to become a certified holistic health coach.

Though losing weight is never the focus of my approach as a health coach, when I committed to eating plant-based myself, I lost weight as a positive side effect. It was a real "aha!" moment when I realized I'd lost thirty pounds without restricting myself or even exercising. My body had recalibrated and naturally detoxed through the power of vitamin- and antioxidant-rich vegetables. My skin was glowing, and I had energy! Gone were the days of needing five cups of coffee to make it through the day. I had proof that this approach to eating *works* in order to bring our bodies back to a more balanced state.

And that brings us to the book you hold in your hands. I wanted to write a book that helped others with similar struggles and celebrated my culinary culture and the culture of so many of my clients. I wanted to remind readers that traditional Caribbean food is actually healthy. If we stripped away all the additives and heavy-meat-low-veggie ratios that have become typical of convenient Puerto Rican cooking, we could get back to the basics and a healthier way to eat.

Not only did I want to honor where I come from, but I wanted to honor the new cultural culinary mash-up I'm creating with my own family. I know this resonates with so many families who start new traditions of their own. My husband Joe comes from a big Italian family and we often cook his family recipes at home, so I even included some of those that we've flipped with plant-based ingredients. Whoever thought pesto had to have Parmesan in it is in for a treat!

For the most part, this book is a collection of recipes that are comforting and familiar and bring me so much joy. They might be very familiar to you, too! In each recipe, I'll show you how to flip classic Puerto Rican and other Latin American and Caribbean dishes. There are even some recipes inspired by American and Italian favorites. Maybe you'll relate to some of the stories I share and, if you're new to plant-based eating, I promise you'll be pleasantly surprised by how easy these recipes are.

I include the nutritional notes of what we'll cook here so that you can really understand how food can fortify your body and reset your natural healing processes. If you're on your own journey to health, I want you to be as informed as possible about the choices you make. Diet culture sends us so many mixed messages about what's "good for us," and I want you to understand how food is fuel, based on science, not some passing fad. I want you to count the colors of your dish, not the calories. I'll teach you how to eat the rainbow with vibrant, vitamin-rich vegetables and use the flavors so integral to Latin cooking so that you don't miss out on anything!

Wherever you are, I know there's something here for you that can change your outlook on healthy eating. Maybe you have a busy life and have relied on convenient prepackaged foods for too long. You may be used to cooking with store-bought broths, spices, and ingredients and have no idea how much needless sodium and sugar are hidden in these products and damaging our health (that was me, too!). Maybe you can't imagine dinner without meat as the centerpiece, but you're really trying to manage your cholesterol. Maybe you're trying to break up with dairy because you feel bloated every time you eat it.

I understand that lifestyle changes are hard and you need all the support you can get. I am here to help you feel better, no matter where you're at. I want this book to be an educational companion as you move toward a life of healthy abundance. Because when we *know* better, we *do* better.

So many of my clients come to me wanting to make a change because they're at risk of developing type 2 diabetes. Countless studies in recent years have pointed to the correlation of a diet high in processed foods, refined sugar, and meat with the risk of developing this disease. My goal is to support my clients in making critical lifestyle changes that can rejuvenate their bodies and spirits. I'm not a doctor, so I can't give medical advice, but my education and experience has taught me that eating more plants is a powerful tool in your toolbox when you are changing daily routines in order to live a longer life. So why not try it?

I am also not a trained chef, but I do come from a long line of women who were self-taught in the kitchen and learned how to cook from their abuelas. This book is for home chefs like you and me. You don't need culinary training to understand how to make incredible recipes that feed your mind, body, and spirit.

The gift of growing up in different culinary worlds with my mom and dad inspired me to find a better way to enjoy the dishes that tie all of us to our culture. I believe we can eat the meals we love, while making healthier choices with upgraded ingredients that pack even more nutrients into the dishes that define who we are. The recipes here are a combination of the recipes from my mom, aunt Tata, and my abuelas. There are even some I've developed from scratch since being a mom and wife myself.

This is the book I wish I had when I was starting my plant-based journey. It will empower you to use vegetables in a different way in your everyday meal prep. You'll master using plant-based ingredients like tofu and will embrace the magic of aquafaba (yes, I will teach you how chickpea water can actually become pudding!). You'll learn that nutritional yeast is an excellent substitute for cheese and how mushrooms will be the new star of your *ropa vieja*. You'll understand what health benefits each vegetable provides through learning about vitamins, minerals, and how your body absorbs them.

Ease into your plant-based lifestyle and use this book as a guide. Since I wrote this for at-home chefs like you and me, I encourage you to have fun with these recipes and add your own personal style and flair. There's no right or wrong with plant-based cooking, so have fun with it!

You'll discover that cooking with vegetables is a little different than cooking with meat. One benefit is that it takes a shorter amount of time, and couldn't we all use a little more of that? At the end of the day, what I really want is for you to use that extra time and these recipes to make memories with your loved ones while you care for yourself.

Make these recipes your own. If you don't have an ingredient, that's okay! You can still make most of these recipes without an ingredient or with substitutions. I've also put together a pantry list to make shopping super easy. It's a list of all the ingredients, spices, and veggies I keep on hand so that I can whip up most of these meals on any given day or night.

You'll notice a lot of ingredient crossover in this book (cilantro, bell peppers, onions, adobo, etc.) so that you can create the Latin flavors you love across many dishes. I think this makes grocery shopping so much easier, and I want that for you. When plant-based cooking becomes easier, it becomes more frequent.

I invite you to try these recipes for ten days and see how you feel. With the new information you learn here, you'll understand why you're making new choices and start changing your mindset from deprivation to abundance. You'll start enjoying food in a whole new way.

You may not think you can go 100 percent plant-based, but I hope this book will help open your mind to eating more vegetables daily. I hope it inspires you to get back to your own roots and see how the cultural dishes you grew up with can be even better with upgraded ingredients that promote a healthy body.

A lot has changed since our grandmothers spent all day in the kitchen preparing meals from scratch. The world has gotten faster and we're certainly busier. We're often reaching for what's convenient instead of nourishing ourselves the way we deserve to be nourished.

My ultimate goal with this book is to inspire you, reader, to slow down and get back to that simpler time, but with all the amazing knowledge you'll soon have about caring for yourself through the power of plants. My wish is that generations of families can sit at the table and enjoy their traditional dishes flipped with high-quality, plant-based ingredients. My wish is that you feed yourself well and open your mind to a kinder, cleaner way of eating. Abuela would be proud.

—Buen provecho.

Love,

Karla (your Latina health coach)

PANTRY MUST-HAVES

These are the key ingredients I always have on hand and that we'll use again and again in these recipes. A lot of them do triple duty across recipes, so if you make these ingredients part of your weekly shopping trips, you'll be ready to cook a plant-based meal at a moment's notice.

When I got more serious about cooking for myself, I realized that the right tools in the kitchen made it easier, so I included some of my favorite kitchen essentials, too. Keep in mind that you don't always have to have everything available to start cooking. Improvise with what you have and be open to substitutions! I include some suggestions as you read along.

Seasonal fruits
Seasonal vegetables*
Cilantro
Parsley
Basil
Olive oil
Vegan butter
Maple syrup
Onion
Garlic
Tomato sauce
Extra firm tofu
Silken tofu
Tempeh
Green plantains
Ripe plantains
Basmati rice**
Rolled oats
Black beans
Gandules (pigeon peas)
Garbanzos (chickpeas)
Red kidney beans
Lentils
Homemade Puerto Rican
    Sofrito (page 21)
Homemade Adobo (page 18)
Homemade Sazón (page 24)
Homemade Almond Milk
    (page 144)

Homemade Oat Milk (page 145)
Chickpea flour
Salt
Ground cinnamon
Ground black pepper
Ground turmeric
Garlic powder
Dried oregano
Dried bay leaves
Red pepper flakes
Nutritional yeast
Raw cashews
Raw almonds
Raw walnuts
Dairy-free milk
Vanilla extract
Coconut palm sugar or brown
    sugar
Chia seeds
Apple cider vinegar
Tahini
Dairy-free chocolate chips
Oat flour
All-purpose flour
Full-fat coconut milk
Spanish olives
Avocado
Sourdough bread
Tamari or soy sauce

---

* Buying vegetables in season means that they are fresher and more flavorful. I try to base my cooking on what is in season and go to the farmers' market when I can.
** I love basmati rice because it's easy to work with and has a delicious nutty flavor. Feel free to use your rice of choice; just watch the cooking time and water-to-rice ratio.

KITCHEN ESSENTIALS

Mixing bowls in various sizes
Serving plates and bowls in
    various sizes
Cooking spoons
Cutting knives
Cutting boards
Whisk
Blender and food processor
Storage containers with lids (I
    use mason jars)
Pot and pans
Measuring cups and spoons

Baking pans
Pie dish
Baking dish
Baking sheets
Loaf pan
Fine mesh strainer
Nut milk bag
Potato masher
Tostonera or lemon squeezer
Box grater
Electric hand mixer or stand
    mixer

Condimentos
(Condiments)

Aquafaba

MAKES: 2–4 SERVINGS | PREP TIME: 10 MINUTES | COOKING TIME: 0 MINUTES

Aquafaba is a wonderful plant-based invention that is going to change your cooking game in a major way, so get ready! Quite literally translated, this "bean water" comes from canned garbanzo beans. It might sound strange, but aquafaba actually mimics the consistency of egg whites. When you learn to work with it (it's easy, I promise), it will be a key ingredient in flipping dessert and batter recipes into healthier versions. Here's a quick breakdown of how I use it: unwhipped aquafaba is great for cookies or mayonnaise; whipped aquafaba can be used for French toast and waffles; and super whipped aquafaba can even be used to make meringues and macaroons. Who knew? Now *you* do. And when we know better, we *do* better.

INGREDIENTS

3½ cups aquafaba from 1 (15-ounce) can chickpeas (save the chickpeas to use in recipes like Chickpea Patties on page 42 and Garbanzos Guisados on page 81)

¼ teaspoon cream of tartar

INSTRUCTIONS

1. Add the aquafaba and cream of tartar to a large mixing bowl.

2. Using an electric hand mixer or stand mixer, mix on high until the mixture forms stiff peaks, about 3 to 5 minutes. *This process takes time, so be patient with it.*

3. Once the aquafaba has reached the right consistency, it's ready to use.

Put your new skills to the test in the Aquafaba French Toast (page 35) and Mayo Ketchup (page 27) recipes.

Balsamic Dressing

MAKES: 2–4 SERVINGS | PREP TIME: 5 MINUTES | COOKING TIME: 0 MINUTES

This oil-free dressing is packed with flavor and adds a nice kick to salads and roasted veggies. If you like using oil in your dressings, I recommend olive oil for its anti-inflammatory properties rather than corn or vegetable oil. The slightly creamy consistency in this dressing is thanks to a touch of nutritional yeast. If you haven't used nutritional yeast yet, the more you cook plant-based, the more you'll rely on it! Nutritional yeast has a savory, nutty, and cheesy flavor that works wonders as a cheese alternative. It's grown specifically to use as a food product and comes in the form of a flakey powder; the yeast cells are killed during the manufacturing process. I love that it's chock-full of nutrients, too, like vitamin B-12, which keeps your blood and nerve cells healthy and can help prevent anemia.

INGREDIENTS

1 teaspoon nutritional yeast

1 teaspoon balsamic vinegar

1 teaspoon Dijon mustard

½–1 teaspoon salt

½ teaspoon dried oregano

¼ teaspoon red pepper flakes (optional)

¼ cup water

INSTRUCTIONS

1. Add all ingredients to a bowl and whisk to combine.

2. Transfer the dressing to an airtight container and keep in the refrigerator for up to a week.

Caldo de Vegetables
(Vegetable Broth)

MAKES: 8–10 CUPS | PREP TIME: 15 MINUTES | COOKING TIME: 2 HOURS 5 MINUTES

Making homemade veggie broth might seem like a chore (I know, grabbing it from the store may be tempting when your schedule is crazy), but the benefits of going homemade are so worth it. The freshness of your broth will pack more nutrients which can reduce inflammation and heal any gut issues. Plus, you'll be avoiding the unnecessary sodium and additives that come with prepackaged versions. It's a win-win *and* you can customize your broth according to your taste.

I gather scraps and freeze them as I cook throughout the week—you can gather scraps from the recipes in this book. Get creative with what you throw in here! I would skip on broccoli, cauliflower, and Brussels sprouts because they can make broth bitter, and potatoes can dilute the flavor and make your broth cloudy, but most everything else is fair game.

INGREDIENTS

3 cups frozen vegetable scraps

2–3 celery stalks, chopped

2 carrots, chopped

5 cloves garlic, peeled

1 red onion, ends removed and cut in half

1 yellow onion, ends removed and cut in half

2–3 dried bay leaves

10–12 cups filtered water

INSTRUCTIONS

1. Add the frozen vegetable scraps to a large pot over medium heat. Let the heat sweat the vegetables for 3 to 5 minutes.

2. Add the remaining ingredients and stir to combine.

3. Bring to a boil, then reduce the heat to a simmer and cook for 1 hour.

4. Once the vegetable broth is ready, carefully remove from the heat and let cool.

5. Set the containers you will use to store the vegetable broth on a flat, sturdy surface. Place a mesh strainer or thin towel over the mouth of the containers and carefully pour in the broth.

6. When finished, discard the cooked vegetables and scraps or, even better, compost them!

7. Store the broth in the fridge for up to a week or freeze for up to a month.

Cashew Condensed Milk

MAKES: 1½ CUPS | PREP TIME: 10 MINUTES | COOKING TIME: 0 MINUTES

Soaked cashews, also known as *marañones*, are another wonderful ingredient that will change how you cook and save you money at the grocery store. After cashews are soaked in water, they can be used as a cream substitute, as the base for cheese-like sauces, and they can even be turned into condensed "milk." I'm big on using this cashew milk for sweet recipes, including a whipped topping for Aquafaba French Toast (page 35) or drizzled over Cranberry and Avena Cookies (page 130).

When you blend cashews in a food processor, the consistency is soft and creamy, and you'll be surprised that it doesn't overpower in flavor when combined with other ingredients. This recipe is a great substitute for sugary, dairy-based condensed milk because cashews are so low in sugar and rich in fiber and plant protein. They're also a good source of copper, magnesium, and manganese, all nutrients that are all important for brain health, immunity, and healthy bones.

INGREDIENTS

¾ cup cashews soaked in hot water for 1–2 hours

½ cup maple syrup

¼ cup coconut butter

2 tablespoons lemon juice

1 tablespoon water

1 teaspoon vanilla extract

⅛ teaspoon salt

INSTRUCTIONS

1. Add all ingredients to a blender and blend on high until smooth and creamy.

2. Transfer the mixture to an airtight container and keep in the refrigerator for up to a week.

Cilantro Chimichurri

MAKES: 1 CUP | PREP TIME: 10 MINUTES | COOKING TIME: 0 MINUTES

Aromatic and herbal, the scent of fresh chimichurri may bring to mind grilled meats because that's how it's typically used in Argentine and Uruguayan steakhouses. It's been adapted by Puerto Rican and Dominican communities and is sometimes called *guasacaca*. You can enjoy the cilantro-rich flavor of this sauce on so many dishes *sin carne* (like juicy Grilled Cauliflower Steaks on page 82). Chimichurri is packed with nutrients thanks to antioxidant-rich cilantro and vitamin-rich garlic. These star ingredients are anti-inflammatory and help prevent infection. Garlic alone has vitamin B-6, manganese, selenium, vitamin C, iron . . . the list goes on and on. And thanks to the heavy dose of parsley in this recipe, you get the benefit of vitamin K, a nutrient that's good for bones, healing wounds, and the appearance of younger-looking skin (bonus!). Best of all, this recipe takes just under ten minutes to make.

INGREDIENTS

½ cup cilantro, chopped

4 cloves garlic, minced

½ cup parsley, chopped

½ cup olive oil

1½ teaspoons red pepper flakes

¼ teaspoon salt

¼ cup apple cider vinegar

INSTRUCTIONS

1. Add all ingredients to a blender and blend on high until smooth. Taste and add more salt if needed.

2. Transfer to an airtight container and keep in the refrigerator for up to a week.

If you have really wilted cilantro, you can dunk a bunch in ice water for ten minutes and it'll perk right up.

Cilantro Dressing

MAKES: 1 CUP | PREP TIME: 5 MINUTES | COOKING TIME: 0 MINUTES

My aunt Tata created this dressing recipe and everyone in the family loves it. She still makes huge batches and hands them out. It's super healthy, thanks to plenty of cilantro and olive oil—both have antioxidants that boost your immunity and reduce inflammation in your body. Paired with the infection-fighting magic of garlic, this dressing makes salads an even healthier choice (and you thought that wasn't possible!). I encourage you to get creative with this one, too. Think outside the salad! I've used this dressing like *sofrito* as a base for stews, rice, and other Latin dishes. I've even added it to some of my husband's pastas and my Loaded Sweet Potato Nachos (page 88). The possibilities are endless, so have fun with it.

INGREDIENTS

1 bunch fresh cilantro

1 cup olive oil

2–3 cloves garlic

INSTRUCTIONS

1. Place all ingredients in a blender and blend on high until smooth.

2. Transfer the mixture to a glass jar or container and cover with a tight lid. Keep in the refrigerator for up to a week.

Store your cilantro in a mason jar with an inch or two of water to keep it fresh for up to a week.

Citrus Salad Dressing

MAKES: 2–4 SERVINGS | PREP TIME: 5 MINUTES | COOKING TIME: 0 MINUTES

Since I use lemons as much as possible (in water, as garnish, etc.) I always have them around. I wanted to create a salad dressing that used my lingering lemons while saving me money at the grocery store. Plus, store-bought dressings can be loaded with sugars and additives, so I always prefer homemade. Lemons naturally boost your immunity and are an awesome source of vitamin C, which is why they're used in homemade medicine along with honey for the common cold—second only to vapor rub! Citric acid from lemons can increase absorption of minerals from other foods. If you get bored of salads easily (I've been there, too), you'll love this tart and slightly sweet dressing.

INGREDIENTS

3 tablespoons olive oil

Juice of 1 lemon

1 tablespoon apple cider vinegar

1 teaspoon Dijon mustard

1 teaspoon dried oregano

½ teaspoon salt

¼ teaspoon ground black pepper

¼ cup water

INSTRUCTIONS

1. Add all ingredients to a bowl and whisk to combine.

2. Transfer to an airtight container and keep in the refrigerator for up to a week.

Don't have lemons on hand? No problem. You can use limes for this dressing and it's just as healthy and offers the same tangy flavor.

Homemade Adobo

MAKES: 7 TABLESPOONS | PREP TIME: 5 MINUTES | COOKING TIME: 0 MINUTES

This all-purpose seasoning is a simple blend of spices that magically adds flavor (and powerful health benefits) to so many savory Caribbean and Latin dishes. You'll see it pop up again and again in this book, so I wanted to give you a recipe to make your own. Store-bought adobo can have additives and preservatives, so this version is not only healthier, but also better for your budget. Adobo features turmeric, a plant native to southeast Asia and India that has been used for centuries in cooking and medicine. Turmeric is a potent anti-inflammatory that can also improve heart health, so you can feel good every time you season your dishes with this homemade adobo.

INGREDIENTS

1 teaspoon ground turmeric

4 tablespoons garlic powder

2 tablespoons salt

2 teaspoons ground black pepper

2 teaspoons dried oregano

INSTRUCTIONS

1. Mix all ingredients together in a small bowl.

2. Transfer to a glass container and seal tight with a lid.

Homemade Puerto Rican Sofrito

MAKES: 1 CUP | PREP TIME: 10 MINUTES | COOKING TIME: 0 MINUTES

Making *sofrito* brings back so many memories of my childhood. In our house, we'd spend an afternoon whipping up sofrito and everyone had a task. My philosophy on going homemade asks the question: Why get store-bought when you can take the time to make your own sofrito (and memories) with loved ones? This is the secret sauce in many Caribbean dishes, especially in Puerto Rico. The aromatic bell peppers, cilantro, garlic, and onion bring out its beautiful flavors. The fresh ingredients used here are a powerhouse of nutrition. Bell peppers have more vitamin C than oranges, garlic is antibacterial, and both onions and cilantro help fight inflammation.

INGREDIENTS

½ green bell pepper, seeds removed

½ red bell pepper, seeds removed

1 bunch fresh cilantro, stems removed

½ bulb garlic, cloves peeled

½ yellow onion, peeled and cut into thick chunks

½ cup olive oil

INSTRUCTIONS

1. Place all ingredients in a blender and blend on high until smooth.

2. Transfer the sofrito into freezer-safe containers and freeze until ready to use.

If you work, making fresh sofrito at home is often way too time-consuming. Instead, make a batch and freeze it by scooping it into ice trays. Then, pop the sofrito cubes into a big resealable freezer bag to thaw as needed. Each cube equals about 1 tablespoon. ¡Tan facil!

Homemade Salad Dressing

MAKES: 2–4 SERVINGS | PREP TIME: 10 MINUTES | COOKING TIME: 0 MINUTES

Fact: The more plant-based you eat, the more veggies you'll need to use up each week. In an effort to be more mindful of food waste, my dad's partner, Somja, taught me how to make this bright, lime-infused dressing that uses the half-cut tomatoes, lingering garlic gloves, and wilting cilantro you probably already have in your fridge by the end of the week. Instead of pitching them, use them in this flavorful recipe. It's so tasty, I even drizzle it over rice sometimes. I recommend red onions here not just because they have a nice, subtly sweet taste in salads, but because they are high in vitamins C, B, and potassium. Red onions are also rich in anthocyanins, which gives them their pretty purple color, a powerful plant pigment that may protect against heart disease, certain cancers, and diabetes. Cheers to your health!

INGREDIENTS

Juice of 1 lime

½ cup tomatoes, chopped

1–2 clove(s) garlic, minced

¼ cup fresh cilantro, chopped

¼ cup red onion, chopped

⅓ cup extra virgin olive oil

⅔ cup filtered water

½ teaspoon salt

¼ teaspoon ground black pepper

½ teaspoon dried oregano

INSTRUCTIONS

1. Add all ingredients to a mason jar, seal tight with a lid, and shake to combine.

2. Use immediately or keep in the refrigerator for up to a week.

Homemade Sazón

MAKES: 5 TABLESPOONS | PREP TIME: 5 MINUTES | COOKING TIME: 0 MINUTES

Like adobo, *sazón* is a key ingredient in any Caribbean and Latin kitchen. It adds a rich, tangy flavor to cooked veggies, rice and more, thanks to the combination of garlic powder, cumin, annatto, and coriander. Garlic is naturally antimicrobial and antibacterial and many folks I know pop garlic pills to get the benefits when it's much tastier (and easier!) to get into the habit of adding it to meals. Annatto is a natural food coloring that comes from the achiote tree, native to South and Central America, and is a popular ingredient in Latin *masa*, or dough. Keep your sazón pure by making your own with fresh spices. I store mine in mini mason jars on the countertop for easy access—and it looks so cute, too!

INGREDIENTS

1 tablespoon garlic powder

1 tablespoon ground cumin

1 tablespoon ground annatto

1 tablespoon ground coriander

1 tablespoon salt

2 teaspoons dried oregano

INSTRUCTIONS

1. Mix all ingredients together in a small bowl.

2. Transfer to a glass container and seal tight with a lid.

Joe's Marinara Sauce

MAKES: 5 CUPS | PREP TIME: 15 MINUTES | COOKING TIME: 50 MINUTES

My husband Joe comes from a big Italian family and Sunday dinner is a can't-miss event at their house. They grocery shop all week to prepare, even if that means traveling to out-of-the-way Italian specialty stores for the very best ingredients. Needless to say, they take their Sunday dinners very seriously and their marinara, or "Sunday gravy," seriously, too. This recipe has been passed down through generations and we love to make it at home because it's all-natural, plant-based, and meat-free. The main ingredients here are tomatoes, a major source of the antioxidant lycopene which has several health benefits and is linked to reducing the risk of heart disease and even some cancers. The tradition of using tomatoes in a gravy, sauce, or *passata* after a bountiful harvest dates back centuries in Italy and has spread across Latin America, too, especially in countries with Italian influence like Argentina. Tomatoes provide essential vitamins like C and K along with folate and potassium. I love the garlicky aroma of this marinara as it simmers on the stove. It reminds me that though we come from totally different backgrounds, Joe and I are preserving our cultural dishes within our own family. I also love that when the "Sunday gravy" is on, it means he's cooking!

INGREDIENTS

4 tablespoons olive oil

1 cup yellow onion, chopped

4 cloves garlic, chopped

3 (12-ounce) cans crushed tomatoes

1 carrot, peeled and cut lengthwise

1 (6-ounce) can tomato paste

⅓ cup fresh basil, chopped

Salt and ground black pepper to taste

INSTRUCTIONS

1. Heat the olive oil in a saucepan over high heat.

2. Add the onions and reduce the heat to medium and sauté until translucent, about 4 to 5 minutes.

3. Add the garlic and combine. Allow the garlic to cook for 1 to 2 minutes, watching it carefully so it doesn't brown.

4. Add the crushed tomatoes and the carrot and mix to combine.

5. Once the sauce comes to a rigorous boil, lower the heat to a simmer.

6. Add the tomato paste, basil, salt, and pepper and let cook for 35 to 40 minutes, stirring occasionally.

7. Once ready, remove from heat and let cool.

8. Once cool, carefully distribute the sauce into containers and store in the refrigerator for up to a week or in the freezer for up to a month.

Mayo Ketchup

MAKES: 2–4 SERVINGS | PREP TIME: 5 MINUTES | COOKING TIME: 0 MINUTES

Growing up in Puerto Rico, mayo ketchup was a standard in our house. I loved dipping French fries and Sorullitos de Maiz (page 107) in this irresistible and easy-to-make dipping sauce. Now that I'm a mom, I've upgraded this traditional favorite that reminds me of home with cleaner ingredients. Next time you're shopping, look for naturally sweetened ketchup without preservatives and mayonnaise without canola oil. This sauce is especially delicious on empanadas, tacos, and arepas. My daughter loves to dip literally anything in this sauce, and I let her, because I know our version is made from clean ingredients.

INGREDIENTS

3 tablespoons ketchup

2 tablespoons vegan mayonnaise

1 clove garlic, minced

½ teaspoon salt

INSTRUCTIONS

1. Add all the ingredients to a small mixing bowl and whisk to combine.

2. Transfer to a glass container, seal tight with a lid, and keep in the fridge for up to a week.

Pesto Sauce

MAKES: 1 CUP | PREP TIME: 10 MINUTES | COOKING TIME: 0 MINUTES

My husband's family always grows vegetables in the summer. They have tomatoes, peppers, and eggplant and always a huge basil plant, which they use to season all of their recipes. When there's just too much basil, they pick the leaves and gather in the kitchen to make a batch of pesto. Now, Joe and I have our own pesto tradition with this plant-based version. Of course, our pesto is best when we can use some of that homegrown basil from his family. Pesto is a traditional savory Italian paste made from basil, garlic, Parmesan cheese, olive oil, and pine nuts. It's super creamy and delicious on everything from pasta to toast to soups. Our version skips the cheese and uses nutritional yeast instead. High in B-12, nutritional yeast is deactivated yeast with a nutty, cheesy flavor you will love. Basil is great for digestion, gut health, and liver health, plus it brightens up any dish with a pretty pop of color and nice aroma.

INGREDIENTS

2 cups fresh basil, long stems removed

½ cup pine nuts or walnuts

2 tablespoons lemon juice

1 clove garlic

3 tablespoons nutritional yeast

¼ teaspoon salt

¼ teaspoon ground black pepper

¼ cup olive oil or more for a smoother consistency

INSTRUCTIONS

1. Add basil, pine nuts, lemon juice, garlic, nutritional yeast, salt, and pepper to a food processor and pulse until a paste is formed.

2. With the food processor running, add the olive oil and pulse until combined. Add more olive oil 1 tablespoon at a time for a smoother consistency. Taste and adjust flavors if needed.

3. Use immediately or transfer to a glass container, seal tight with a lid, and keep in the fridge for up to a week.

Tahini Dressing

MAKES: ¾ CUP | PREP TIME: 5 MINUTES | COOKING TIME: 0 MINUTES

My aunt Tata and uncle Soto used this tahini dressing recipe on the popular veggie sandwiches they served at their restaurant. The nutty, creamy taste takes me right back to sitting at the corner table enjoying subs with fake "deli meat" (now I steer clear of processed fake meats, but as a kid I *loved* them), alfalfa sprouts, and this amazing dressing. Once you start making tahini dressing, you'll be amazed at how you'll use it on everything from roasted veggies to salads and sandwiches. Not only is it a versatile dressing you'll always want to have in the fridge, but it's also high in healthy fats and amino acids. The essential vitamins and minerals found in tahini may even help regulate blood pressure and cholesterol.

INGREDIENTS

¼ cup warm water or more for a smoother consistency

½ cup tahini (ground sesame seeds)

1 clove garlic, minced

Juice of 1 lemon

¼ teaspoon salt

INSTRUCTIONS

1. Add all ingredients to a bowl and whisk to combine. Add more warm water 1 tablespoon at a time for a smoother consistency.

2. Use immediately or transfer to a glass container, seal tight with a lid, and keep in the fridge for up to a week.

Tofu Ricotta "Cheese"

MAKES: 2 CUPS | PREP TIME: 10 MINUTES | COOKING TIME: 0 MINUTES

A lot of my clients tell me they never cook with tofu because they think it has no flavor. I get it, tofu can taste flavorless, but that's only because people don't know how to prepare it! It needs some tender love and care to truly stand out in your cooking (and trust me, it will once you start learning how to use it). Like with most dishes you make, the key to cooking tofu is to flavor it with plenty of seasonings and sauces that you love. When you season your plant-based meals well, you don't even miss the meat. Tofu ricotta is the easiest thing to make, and you can use it in several ways. Even my husband is a tofu ricotta convert! He uses it in Eggplant Parm (page 78). None of us miss the ricotta (we don't think you will either). You can even spread it on toast with fresh lemon zest and black pepper. If you have any reservations about tofu, I think this "cheese" will change your mind.

INGREDIENTS

1 (14-ounce) block extra firm tofu, drained but not pressed

Juice of 1 lemon

2 tablespoons nutritional yeast

¼ cup fresh parsley

1 teaspoon red pepper flakes

½ teaspoon salt

INSTRUCTIONS

1. Place all ingredients in a food processor and pulse until well combined and smooth. Taste and adjust seasonings as needed by adding more salt and/or red pepper flakes.

2. Use immediately or transfer to a glass container, seal tight with a lid, and keep in the fridge for up to a week.

Desayunos y Brunch
(Breakfast and Brunch)

Aquafaba French Toast
with Parcha Cream

MAKES: 6–8 SERVINGS | PREP TIME: 15 MINUTES | COOKING TIME: 15 MINUTES

The flavor of passion fruit, or *parcha*, immediately takes me back to my childhood in Puerto Rico. Whenever I ordered shaved ice, or *piragua*, I never wanted tamarind, coconut, or any other flavor. I always went for the sweet-but-tart passion fruit. In this recipe, the passion fruit topping balances the sweetness of the French toast and gives it a kick of vitamin A, which is great for skin and vision. Plus, it has vitamin C, a crucial antioxidant for your immune system. Not a passion fruit fan? You can substitute whatever citrus fruit you like! Not only can you customize the fruit flavors here, but you'll get experience using whipped Aquafaba (page 7) to replace the egg. My daughter loves this upgraded take on French toast so much, she can't tell the difference.

INGREDIENTS

French Toast

2 cups aquafaba (page 7)

1 cup dairy-free milk

1 teaspoon vanilla extract

½ teaspoon ground cinnamon, plus more for serving

8 slices sourdough bread or whole wheat bread

Parcha Cream

½ cup plain, dairy-free yogurt

1–1½ tablespoons passion fruit puree

1 tablespoon maple syrup

To Serve

Fruit of choice (banana, mango, pineapple, etc.)

Maple syrup

Lime zest to garnish

INSTRUCTIONS

1. To make the French toast, add the aquafaba, milk, vanilla, and cinnamon to a shallow bowl and stir to combine. Set aside.

2. Spray a skillet with nonstick cooking spray and place over medium heat.

3. Dip both sides of each bread slice into the aquafaba mixture and place in the skillet to cook for 2 to 3 minutes. Turn over gently, then cook for another 2 to 3 minutes or until golden brown. Repeat with the remaining slices of bread.

4. To make the parcha cream, add the yogurt, passion fruit puree, and maple syrup to a bowl and whisk to combine.

5. Serve the French toast warm with a nice helping of parcha cream, fruit, maple syrup, a sprinkle of cinnamon, and lime zest.

Baked Oatmeal

MAKES: 2–4 SERVINGS | PREP TIME: 15 MINUTES | COOKING TIME: 25 MINUTES

Both of my abuelas made the best *avena* (oatmeal). Latin-style oatmeal is made with milk, sugar, cinnamon, and vanilla. Some families make it soupier than others but both of my abuelas made it on the less soupy side and it was so rich and comforting. I will always remember Abuela cozying up next to the stove as she stirred her oatmeal with a metal spoon until it was just the right consistency. The smell of freshly made avena will live with me forever and brings me a lot of joy. Since oats are such a rich source of healthy carbs and fiber and pack more protein than other grains, they're an awesome option for breakfast. This version is a little different. It uses all the fresh ingredients from Abuela's kitchen with the addition of fiber-rich chia and flax seeds, banana, berries, and coconut. Plus, it cuts the time spent stirring because you just pop it in the oven and bake it (the cinnamon aroma that will fill your house is an added bonus)!

INGREDIENTS

1 banana, mashed

½ cup rolled oats

⅔ cup dairy-free milk

2 teaspoons chia seeds

2 teaspoons ground flax seeds

⅛ teaspoon salt

½ cup frozen berries

¼ cup shredded coconut

To Serve

Dairy-free yogurt

Maple syrup

INSTRUCTIONS

1. Preheat the oven to 350°F. Spray a 9 x 9-inch baking dish with nonstick cooking spray and set aside.

2. To a mixing bowl, add the mashed banana, oats, dairy-free milk, seeds, and salt and combine.

3. Pour the mixture into the baking pan and top with frozen berries and shredded coconut. Place in the oven to bake for 20 to 25 minutes or until the edges start to turn golden brown.

4. Once ready, remove from the oven.

5. Serve with dairy-free yogurt and a drizzle of maple syrup and enjoy!

Carrot Cake Muffins

MAKES: 12 MUFFINS | PREP TIME: 15 MINUTES | COOKING TIME: 30 MINUTES

In our house, making these muffins is a family activity. We've started a bit of a tradition where we whip these up on weekends when it feels like we have endless time together. It's such a treat for my daughter to mix the ingredients and I love showing her how simple it is to make baked goods with completely plant-based ingredients. When you think about it, it's kind of magical that the star ingredient of her favorite sweet muffin is actually a carrot! Carrots are awesome for many reasons, mainly because they're an excellent source of beta carotene, which your body converts to vitamin A, a vital nutrient for healthy skin and good vision. This versatile veggie is also a great source of B vitamins and potassium.

INGREDIENTS

2 cups rolled oats

¼ cup flax seeds

2 teaspoons baking powder

½ teaspoon baking soda

½ teaspoon salt

2 teaspoons ground cinnamon

½ teaspoon ground ginger

1½ cups dairy-free milk

⅓ cup cashew butter

¼ cup brown sugar

½ cup applesauce

2 medium-size carrots, chopped

1 tablespoon lemon juice

1 teaspoon vanilla

¾ cup raisins

1 cup coarsely chopped walnuts

INSTRUCTIONS

1. Preheat the oven to 350°F. Line a muffin tin with muffin liners, spray with nonstick cooking spray, and set aside.

2. To a blender add the oats, flax seeds, baking powder, baking soda, salt, cinnamon, and ginger and blend on high to combine.

3. To the same blender add the dairy-free milk, cashew butter, sugar, applesauce, carrots, lemon juice, and vanilla and blend on high to combine.

4. Pour the mixture in a large mixing bowl and fold in the raisins and walnuts.

5. Evenly divide the batter into the muffin liners and bake for 25 to 30 minutes or until a toothpick inserted comes out mostly clean.

6. Remove from the oven and let cool before serving.

Chia Pudding
Topped with Papaya and Piña

MAKES: 2–4 SERVINGS | PREP TIME: 5 MINUTES | COOKING TIME: 0 MINUTES

When people tell me they want an easy, no-fuss breakfast (working parents, I'm looking at you!), I recommend this recipe. If you haven't made chia pudding before, you're in for a treat. Chia seeds are a great way to start your day since they are loaded with fiber and protein. These little seeds are superfoods that may help reduce insulin levels, too. Both papaya and pineapple have bromelain and papain, enzymes that help digest food and provide other potential health benefits. Made with dairy-free milk, this pudding is a super healthy breakfast that satisfies a sweet tooth. It's the best of both worlds.

INGREDIENTS

½ cup chia seeds

2 cups dairy-free milk, unsweetened

2 tablespoons maple syrup, plus more for serving

1 teaspoon vanilla extract

⅛ teaspoon salt

To Serve

Fresh papaya cubes

Fresh pineapple cubes

Maple syrup for drizzling

INSTRUCTIONS

1. In a glass container, add the chia seeds, dairy-free milk, maple syrup, vanilla, and salt and whisk to combine. Cover and place in the refrigerator for 4 to 6 hours or overnight to set.

2. Once ready, remove the chia pudding from the refrigerator. Serve with fresh papaya and pineapple cubes and maple syrup.

Chickpea Patties

MAKES: 4–6 SERVINGS | PREP TIME: 15 MINUTES | COOKING TIME: 15 MINUTES

High in protein and with a "meaty" texture, chickpea patties are a fiber- and vitamin-rich substitute for meat. Chickpeas have magnesium, B vitamins, and selenium. They even offer iron, which is great if you're transitioning from animal protein. This recipe uses garlic and Homemade Adobo (page 18), so the patties are super flavorful. Then, they're fried in olive oil to get a crispy texture. ¡Que rico! You can serve these patties with almost anything. I love them on salads, inside sandwiches, even served solo with a side of roasted veggies. Next time you have a craving for a burger, try these chickpea patties instead and load them up with your favorite toppings (you won't miss the meat).

INGREDIENTS

1 (15-ounce) can chickpeas, drained and rinsed (save the liquid to make Aquafaba French Toast on page 35)

½ celery stalk, diced

½ cup shredded carrot

½ cup chopped yellow onion

1 clove garlic, minced

¼ cup oat flour

1 teaspoon Homemade Adobo (page 18)

½ teaspoon salt

½ teaspoon ground black pepper

2–3 tablespoons olive oil for frying

INSTRUCTIONS

1. Add the chickpeas to a large mixing bowl. Using a potato masher or the back of a fork, mash the chickpeas until they are broken down into smaller pieces.

2. Add the celery, carrot, onion, garlic, oat flour, adobo, salt, and pepper and combine. If the mixture is too loose, add 1 tablespoon of water at a time until the mixture becomes a bit stickier.

3. Using clean hands, scoop the chickpea mixture to form two-inch wide patties.

4. Heat the olive oil in a pan or skillet over medium heat. Add the patties and cook for 3 to 4 minutes on each side or until golden brown.

5. Serve immediately and enjoy!

Classic VLT

MAKES: 2–4 SERVINGS | PREP TIME: 15 MINUTES | COOKING TIME: 35 MINUTES

When I was a kid visiting Puerto Rico, sometimes my aunt Tata and uncle Soto made me a meatless BLT (bacon, lettuce, and tomato) sandwich. They'd use a prepackaged bacon substitute that was available in the nineties, but there have been major advancements in plant-based cooking since then. Enter "vacon," or vegan bacon! That's the "v" in this sandwich recipe that I think will surprise and delight you. Vacon is a bacon substitute made from shiitake mushrooms, and cooked with tamari, liquid smoke, and maple syrup to give it a salty, well, *bacon*-like flavor. It's great in a sandwich or served with my Garbanzo Flour Omelet (page 46). The best part? You'll feel great eating shiitake vacon because these mushrooms support immune health and are naturally anti-inflammatory.

INGREDIENTS

Vacon

2 cups shiitake mushrooms, sliced and stems removed

1 tablespoon olive oil

2 teaspoons tamari or soy sauce

1½ teaspoon maple syrup

1 teaspoon liquid smoke

½ teaspoon ground black pepper

To Serve

1–2 tablespoons Mayo Ketchup (page 27)

4 slices sourdough bread, toasted

2–4 pieces green leaf lettuce

½ ripe tomato, thinly sliced

¼ red onion, thinly sliced

½ ripe avocado, pitted, peeled, and sliced

INSTRUCTIONS

1. To make the vacon, preheat oven to 350°F. Line a baking sheet with parchment paper and set it aside.

2. To a large mixing bowl, add the shiitake mushrooms, olive oil, tamari or soy sauce, maple syrup, liquid smoke, and pepper and combine. Spread the mushrooms evenly on the lined baking sheet and bake for 30 to 35 minutes, tossing halfway until the mushrooms are dried and slightly crispy. Remove from the oven and set aside.

Use a damp cloth to wipe the mushrooms clean (if you wash them in water, they will not become crisp in the oven).

3. To assemble the sandwiches, spread Mayo Ketchup on 2 slices of toasted sourdough bread. Top each slice with lettuce, tomato, onion, avocado slices, and vacon, then close the sandwiches with the remaining bread. Serve immediately and enjoy!

Fish-Free Ceviche

Ceviche, or citrus-cured fish, originated in Peru but is also popular in the Caribbean. The Peruvian version often uses sea bass and is served with potatoes and corn. In Puerto Rican ceviche, shrimp, squid, or snapper is used, but in this recipe, *zero* seafood is used. Yes, you can still enjoy the bold, refreshing flavors of ceviche with this totally plant-based version! Hearts of palm are perfect for replacing the fish. They have a firm, fleshy texture that mimics fish and they offer a healthy dose of plant protein with properties that aid digestion. A marinade of jalapeño, cilantro, red onion, and olive oil make this the perfect summer dish for a hot day.

INGREDIENTS

2 (14-ounce) cans whole hearts of palm, drained and cut into ½-inch slices

1 cup cherry tomatoes, quartered

½ small red onion, finely diced

¼ cup fresh lime juice (about 2–3 limes)

1 cup avocado chunks

½ cup fresh cilantro, chopped

1 jalapeño, finely diced and seeds removed (optional)

1 teaspoon kelp granules (optional)

Salt and pepper to taste

To Serve

Grain-free or corn tortillas

INSTRUCTIONS

1. To a large mixing bowl, add hearts of palm, cherry tomatoes, red onion, lime juice, avocado, cilantro, jalapeño (if using), and kelp granules (if using) and mix to combine. Season with salt and pepper to taste.

2. Serve with grain-free or corn tortillas and enjoy.

Frituritas de Platano
(Plantain Fritters)

MAKES 2–4 SERVINGS | PREP TIME: 10 MINUTES | COOKING TIME: 10 MINUTES

Anyone who grew up in the Latin community knows that cooked green plantains are delicious and nutritious. Sure, they have a similar calorie count to a potato, but this fruit is a better source of fiber, vitamins A, C, and B-6. If you're like me, you were taught to eat the inside of the plantain (the starchy yellow part) and toss out the peel. But what if I told you that the peel of a green plantain has powerful healing properties, too (mind blown, right)? It's high in vitamin A, which promotes healing of wounds, can speed up cell regeneration, and has skin-softening effects. This fritter recipe uses the whole plantain so you can get all the healthy benefits this superfood offers!

INGREDIENTS

2 medium-sized organic green plantains, unpeeled, washed, and ends removed

½ teaspoon garlic powder

½ teaspoon salt

2 cups olive oil for frying

To Serve

Mayo Ketchup (page 27)

Eating plantain peels can expose you to contaminants or pesticides, so it's important to buy organic when possible or scrub them carefully to remove any harmful toxins. When you know better, you do better.

INSTRUCTIONS

1. Place a box grater over a large mixing bowl and grate the plantains. Add garlic powder and salt and combine.

2. Heat the oil in a large pan or skillet over medium heat.

3. Using clean hands, form 2 x 2-inch patties (about the size of the palm of your hand). Fry for 2 to 3 minutes on each side or until the edges are golden brown and crispy.

4. Remove the patties from the pan and place on a plate lined with a paper towel to help absorb any excess olive oil.

5. Serve with Mayo Ketchup or your favorite dipping sauce and enjoy.

Garbanzo Flour Omelet
with Sauteed Veggies

MAKES: 2–4 SERVINGS | PREP TIME: 10 MINUTES | COOKING TIME: 10 MINUTES

This eggless omelet recipe (yes, I said *eggless omelet*) is proof that you can truly flip any meal into a plant-based alternative. Garbanzo (chickpea) flour, nutritional yeast, and a mixture of dairy-free milk and lemon juice make up the "egg" base here and the spinach filling provides a punch of iron. Garlic salt, onions, and red pepper flakes add a super savory and delicious kick.

I think chickpea flour is an amazing product. Only one cup of it carries more folate than you need in an entire day! It's an important ingredient to cook with if you or your partner are pregnant because folate plays an important role in brain and spine health for a developing baby. I also love that chickpea flour has a gradual effect on blood sugar, thanks to its low glycemic index, which is great if you're managing diabetes.

INGREDIENTS

¾ cup chickpea flour

1 tablespoon nutritional yeast

½ teaspoon baking powder

½ teaspoon garlic powder

¼ teaspoon onion powder

Pinch red pepper flakes

¼ teaspoon sea salt

¾ cup dairy-free milk, unsweetened

1 tablespoon lemon juice

1 tablespoon olive oil or more if needed

To Serve

Veggies of choice

INSTRUCTIONS

1. In a large mixing bowl, combine chickpea flour, nutritional yeast, baking powder, garlic powder, onion powder, red pepper flakes, and salt.

2. To the same mixing bowl, add dairy-free milk and lemon juice and whisk until all ingredients are well combined.

3. Add the olive oil into a pan or skillet and place over medium heat. Pour half of the batter into the pan and lightly spread out the edges. Cook for about 3 to 5 minutes or until bubbles form across the entire surface of the omelet and the batter begins to firm up.

4. Using a spatula, flip and press the surface of the omelet gently and cook for another 1 to 2 minutes until done. Repeat with the remaining batter.

5. Serve the omelets immediately with your favorite veggies.

Kale Salad
with Garbanzo Beans

MAKES: 2–4 SERVINGS | PREP TIME: 15 MINUTES | COOKING TIME: 30 MINUTES

Like spinach, arugula, romaine, and other dark leafy greens, kale is a great source of fiber, folate, and antioxidants, which help strengthen your immune system. I try to incorporate kale into as many of my meals as possible, but I know some people don't like its tough texture. If that's you, here's a trick: treat your kale to a massage! Massaging kale with a healthy fat like olive oil or mashed avocado softens the leaves and takes out any bitter taste. If you don't have a healthy fat on hand, acidic ingredients like lemon or apple cider vinegar do the trick, too. This salad has massaged kale and plenty of crunch thanks to roasted garbanzo beans and seeds. Garbanzo beans, or chickpeas, add a punch of protein and are a staple of Caribbean cooking—you see them a lot in Jamaican dishes, too. I love to add radishes and avocado in this salad, but feel free to add in any extra veggies to customize yours.

INGREDIENTS

1 (16-ounce) can chickpeas, drained and rinsed

1 tablespoon olive oil

1 teaspoon Homemade Adobo (page 18)

1 teaspoon Homemade Sazón (page 24)

3 cups kale, finely chopped and stems removed

1 ripe avocado, divided

½ cup sliced cucumbers

½ cup sliced radishes

¼ cup sliced red onion

Juice of 1 lemon

1 tablespoon sunflower seeds

1 tablespoon pumpkin seeds

Salt and pepper to taste

INSTRUCTIONS

1. Preheat the oven to 400°F. Line a baking sheet with parchment paper and set it aside.

2. To a large mixing bowl, add the chickpeas, olive oil, adobo, and sazón and mix to combine. Spread the chickpeas onto the lined baking sheet and roast for 25 to 30 minutes or until the chickpeas are golden brown and crispy. Remove from the oven and set aside.

3. To another large mixing bowl, add the kale and half of the avocado. Using clean hands or a potato masher, massage the avocado into the kale for 1 to 2 minutes or until the kale softens.

4. Mix in the cucumbers, radishes, onion, lemon juice, seeds, and roasted chickpeas and toss to combine. Season with salt and pepper to taste.

5. Serve with the remaining avocado, sliced, and enjoy!

Mayo-less Potato Salad

MAKES: 2–4 SERVINGS | PREP TIME: 15 MINUTES | COOKING TIME: 20 MINUTES

Is summer really summer without potato salad? Personally, I don't think so. The problem with store-bought mayonnaise (even plant-based) is that it can be packed with additives. So, I flipped a potato salad recipe I love into one that's completely made from scratch with plant-based ingredients. The creamy, dairy-free dressing in this potato salad uses the magical properties of soaked cashews. You can also use this dressing in coleslaw dishes. Since cashews offer fiber, heart-healthy fats, and plant protein, this is an upgraded way to enjoy a classic dish that is sure to make its way to your table during warmer seasons.

INGREDIENTS

1 pound (about 2 cups) small red potatoes, washed and quartered

1 cup raw cashews, soaked in hot water for 1 hour, drained and rinsed

1 clove garlic

1 tablespoon maple syrup

2 teaspoons yellow mustard

1 tablespoon apple cider vinegar

3 tablespoons red onion, chopped

¼ teaspoon salt

¼ teaspoon ground black pepper

⅓ cup water, plus more if needed

INSTRUCTIONS

1. Place a pot over medium-high heat. Add the potatoes and cover with water. Bring the potatoes to a boil, then reduce the heat to a simmer. Cook for 15 to 20 minutes or until tender. Once tender, remove from heat, drain, and let cool.

2. Add the soaked cashews, garlic, maple syrup, mustard, apple cider vinegar, red onion, salt, pepper, and water into a blender and blend on high until smooth and creamy. If too thick, add more water 1 tablespoon at a time.

3. Pour the dressing over the cooked potatoes and mix to combine. Taste and adjust the seasoning if needed.

4. Serve and enjoy!

Mexican-Inspired Corn Salad

MAKES: 4–6 SERVINGS | PREP TIME: 15 MINUTES | COOKING TIME: 15 MINUTES

I know I'm not alone when I say that I'm pretty sure I could eat Mexican food every single day. Which is great news, since so many Mexican dishes I love are plant-based. I especially love *elote*, Mexican street corn. Traditionally, elote has about a bazillion calories along with plenty of cheese, so I played around with a recipe that integrated all the amazing flavors but with plant-based ingredients. This recipe ditches the cheese (crazy, I know), swaps mayonnaise with eggless mayo, and it all gets elevated with oven-roasted jalapeños. The end result? Corn that's smoky, creamy, and healthy enough so that you can enjoy a margarita, too. While working on this recipe for the book, my mom shared an awesome tip as we prepared to chop the garlic. She said her grandma used to soak unpeeled garlic cloves in a covered bowl (for about an hour, she said). It makes the skins slide right off!

INGREDIENTS

1 tablespoon olive oil

2 cloves garlic, minced

4 cups corn kernels, fresh or frozen (thaw if using frozen)

1 roasted jalapeño pepper, chopped and seeds removed

½ cup red onion, chopped

3 tablespoons vegan mayo

Juice of 2 limes

½ cup fresh cilantro, chopped, plus more for serving

½ teaspoon smoked paprika

½ teaspoon dried oregano

Salt and pepper to taste

Lime wedges to garnish

INSTRUCTIONS

1. Heat the olive oil in a pan or skillet over medium heat.

2. Add garlic and corn and sauté until kernels start to brown, about 5 to 7 minutes. Remove from heat and transfer the corn mixture to a large mixing bowl. Add roasted jalapeño pepper, red onion, mayo, lime juice, cilantro, paprika, and oregano and combine.

3. Season with salt and pepper to taste.

4. Serve with more chopped cilantro and lime wedges.

You can roast jalapeño peppers on a gas stove. Turn your gas stove flame on medium and hold pepper over the flame for 60 to 90 seconds or until the skin on one side chars and blisters. Turn the pepper and let the other side roast for another 60 to 90 seconds. Carefully remove from heat and place in a paper bag and seal for 5 to 10 minutes. Remove from the paper bag and peel the charred skin from the pepper. Remove the seeds, chop, and add to the corn salad.

Mushroom Jibaritos
(Plantain Mushroom Sandwich)

MAKES: 2–4 SERVINGS | PREP TIME: 15 MINUTES | COOKING TIME: 20 MINUTES

The origin story of the mushroom *jibarito*, or plantain sandwich, is a tale of flipping recipe ingredients at its best! Some say it was popularized in the United States by Juan Figueroa, a chef at Borinquen Restaurant in Chicago. In the mid-nineties, he read about a sandwich using plantains as bread in Puerto Rico so he created a similar sandwich using steak, tomato, lettuce, and onions and put it on the menu. He named his sandwich the jibarito after the jibaro mountain culture of Puerto Rico. The sandwich was a hit! Prepared in a similar way to tostones, plantains make an excellent bread substitute and offer way more plant-based protein and fiber. This recipe swaps out steak for mushrooms, which have amazing immune-boosting properties. The marinade of liquid smoke and tamari or soy sauce gives the mushrooms an umami-rich taste and dairy-free Mayo Ketchup (page 27) adds a creamy, tangy kick. I love serving this to meat lovers and blowing their minds!

INGREDIENTS

Mushroom Steaks

1 tablespoon olive oil

3 tablespoons Homemade Puerto Rican Sofrito (page 21)

½ yellow onion, thinly sliced

1½ tablespoons tamari or soy sauce

1 teaspoon Homemade Adobo (page 18)

½ teaspoon liquid smoke

¼ cup water

2 large portabella mushrooms, stems removed

Plantains

2 green plantains, peeled and halved

3 cups olive oil for frying

Suggested Toppings

Lettuce

Tomato

Red onion, thinly sliced

Mayo Ketchup (page 27)

INSTRUCTIONS

1. To make the mushroom steaks, heat 1 tablespoon olive oil in a pan over medium heat. Add sofrito and sauté for 1 to 2 minutes.

2. Add in the onion, tamari or soy sauce, adobo, liquid smoke, and water and combine. Let cook until the onions begin to soften.

3. Once the onions start to soften, gently place the mushroom caps over the onions, lower the heat, cover, and let cook for 5 to 7 minutes or until tender. Set aside.

(Continued)

4. To make the plantains, heat 3 cups of olive oil in a large pan or skillet over high heat.

5. Fry the cut plantains until lightly golden but not browned, about 5 to 7 minutes. Transfer to a plate lined with a paper towel to absorb the excess oil.

6. Using the bottom of a heavy plate or pan, flatten each plantain piece to ¼-inch thickness. Return to the hot oil and fry again on each side for 2 to 3 minutes or until golden and crispy on the edges. Remove from oil and place on a plate lined with a paper towel to absorb the excess oil.

7. To build the jibaritos, place one mushroom cap and cooked onions on a slice of fried plantain along with lettuce, tomato, red onion slices, and a generous amount of Mayo Ketchup. Top with another plantain to form a sandwich. Repeat with the remaining mushroom steak and plantains.

8. Serve immediately and enjoy!

Papas, Peppers, and Onions

MAKES: 2–4 SERVINGS | PREP TIME: 50 MINUTES | COOKING TIME: 35 MINUTES

My husband's family is all about their potatoes (*papas*) and peppers, a staple in Italian cooking. They even make a roasted pepper, potato, and egg sandwich, which was new to me! This take on potatoes and peppers uses classic Italian seasonings like oregano and red pepper flakes along with cilantro. You can use any bell peppers you might have lying around, but I like to use orange ones. Fun fact: Did you know that a bell pepper actually has more vitamin C than an orange? You'll also get a nice immune boost from the garlic, cilantro, and parsley in this recipe. *Buon appetito!*

INGREDIENTS

2 large yellow potatoes, chopped into 2-inch squares

3 tablespoons olive oil, divided

½ teaspoon salt

½ teaspoon ground black pepper

½ yellow onion, chopped

1 orange bell pepper, chopped and seeds removed

1 red bell pepper, chopped and seeds removed

2 cloves garlic, minced

½ teaspoon red pepper flakes

½ teaspoon dried oregano

¼ cup fresh cilantro, chopped

¼ cup fresh parsley, chopped

INSTRUCTIONS

1. Preheat the oven to 350°F. Line a baking sheet with parchment paper and set it aside.

2. To a large mixing bowl, add the potatoes, 2 tablespoons of olive oil, salt, and pepper and combine. Transfer the potatoes to your lined baking sheet and roast for 20 minutes or until the edges are golden brown and the insides are tender. Once ready, remove from the oven and set aside.

3. Heat the remaining olive oil in a large pan or skillet. Add the onions and peppers and cook for 7 to 10 minutes or until they start to become tender. Add the minced garlic and cook for 1 to 2 more minutes.

4. Carefully add the roasted potatoes to the pan with the cooked onions and peppers and combine. Add red pepper flakes and dried oregano and mix all ingredients together. Taste and adjust the seasoning by adding more salt and pepper if needed. Once seasoned, turn off the heat. Add fresh cilantro and parsley and combine. Serve and enjoy!

This dish pairs well with the Garbanzo Flour Omelet (page 46) and Tofu Scramble Burrito (page 62).

Parfait de Batata
(Sweet Potato Parfait)

It might sound crazy, but creamy sweet potatoes are a fabulous alternative to dairy yogurt when you have a sweet tooth. I love a yogurt parfait as a treat after dinner or even at breakfast, so when I went plant-based I didn't want to miss out. And turns out, I didn't have to! My daughter loves making this with me, and we have fun customizing our parfaits with our favorite fruit and nuts. This recipe calls for Japanese sweet potatoes, which are naturally high in fiber, antioxidants, and heart-healthy minerals. If you can't find Japanese sweet potatoes at your grocery store or vegetable stand, you can use orange sweet potatoes.

INGREDIENTS

2 large Japanese sweet potatoes, peeled and cubed

⅔ cup maple syrup

1 tablespoon vanilla extract

To Serve

1 ripe mango, peeled and cut into cubes

½ cup fresh blueberries

Fresh mint to garnish (optional)

INSTRUCTIONS

1. Bring a large pot of water to a rolling boil. Carefully add the sweet potatoes to the boiling water and let them cook for 15 to 20 minutes or until tender. Once tender, remove from the heat, strain, and rinse under cold water. Set aside to allow the sweet potatoes to cool completely.

2. Once cooled, transfer the sweet potatoes to a blender. Add maple syrup and vanilla and blend on high until smooth and creamy.

3. To make the parfaits, add a layer of sweet potato cream to cover the bottom of a cup. Top with mango and/or blueberries. Repeat the same arrangement until the cups are full.

4. Garnish with mint leaves if desired and keep refrigerated until ready to enjoy!

Roasted Eggplant Sandwiches
with Tahini Dressing

MAKES: 2–4 SERVINGS | PREP TIME: 20 MINUTES | COOKING TIME: 20 MINUTES

When eggplant is seasoned well and roasted just right, it can feel like you're eating a meaty dish. I love using roasted *berenjenas* (eggplant) as the core ingredient of a sandwich piled high with veggies and drizzled with dressing, but eggplant also makes great plant-based "meatballs" and dips! Fun fact: Did you know that the eggplant, which is most often prepared as a vegetable, is actually a fruit? Because it grows from a flowering plant with seeds, it is indeed a fruit. It's also really healthy, thanks to anthocyanins, which give it its purple color and offer antioxidants that can protect against cellular damage. You can also feel good about eating sourdough bread because it's made with fermented yeast, which is great for gut health.

INGREDIENTS

3 tablespoons tamari or soy sauce

2 tablespoons olive oil

½ teaspoon toasted sesame oil

1-inch piece (about 1 tablespoon) fresh
   ginger, grated

2 cloves garlic, minced

⅓ cup water

1 medium-sized eggplant, peeled and sliced
   into ½-inch rounds

Sandwiches

¼ cup Tahini Dressing (page 29)

4 slices sourdough bread, toasted

Spinach, arugula, or a mixture of both

½ ripe tomato, sliced

¼ red onion, thinly sliced

INSTRUCTIONS

1. Preheat the oven to 400°F. Line a baking sheet with parchment paper and set it aside.

2. To a mixing bowl, add the tamari, oils, ginger, garlic, and water and whisk to combine.

3. Place the sliced eggplant in a flat dish and cover with the marinade. Cover and let marinate in the refrigerator for 15 minutes.

4. Arrange the marinated eggplant slices on the lined baking sheet and place in the oven to roast for 10 minutes. Flip the eggplant, brush with leftover marinade, and roast for 8 to 10 minutes more or until soft and golden. Once ready, remove from the oven and set aside.

5. To assemble the sandwiches, spread a layer of tahini dressing on each slice of toasted sourdough bread and top with greens, tomato, red onion, and roasted eggplant. Close the sandwiches and serve.

Tofu Scramble Burrito

The secret to falling in love with plant-based cooking depends on three things: flavor, flavor, and *flavor*! Seasoning your dishes is crucial, and you'll get great practice with this recipe. Tofu is like a blank slate—it absorbs any flavor you season it with, and the texture is perfect as a scrambled egg substitute. This is a great recipe for tofu newbies to get more comfortable using this super versatile ingredient. Another thing I love about this recipe is that you can really make it your own. Once you get comfortable making a basic scramble, customize it! Try adding dairy-free cheese, switch up the veggies with whatever is in the fridge, or even add black beans for an extra punch of plant protein. Fun fact: Did you know that the roots of the modern-day burrito date back to 10,000 BC? People living in Mesoamerica, now present-day Mexico, commonly used corn tortillas to wrap foods.

INGREDIENTS

Tofu Scramble

1 (14-ounce) block extra firm tofu, drained

1 tablespoon olive oil

½ yellow onion, chopped

1 clove garlic, minced

1 tablespoon Homemade Adobo (page 18) or
    all-purpose seasoning

1 teaspoon ground turmeric

¼ teaspoon salt

¼ teaspoon ground pepper

Burrito Filling

3–4 burrito-size tortillas

Hummus

1 cup fresh spinach, arugula, or a mix of both

½ medium red bell pepper, thinly sliced

½ ripe tomato, sliced

½ cup carrots, shredded

1 ripe avocado, peeled, pitted, and sliced

INSTRUCTIONS

1. Wrap the block of tofu in a clean kitchen towel and set something heavy on top like a cast-iron skillet to press out the excess moisture. Set it aside.

2. Heat the olive oil in a pan or skillet over medium heat. Add the onions and cook until translucent, about 4 to 5 minutes. Add the garlic and adobo and combine.

3. Using clean hands, crumble the tofu into the pan. Add turmeric, salt, and pepper and combine. Let the tofu cook for 2 to 3 minutes to absorb all the flavors. Once ready, remove from heat.

Adding ground turmeric not only boosts flavor and color, making the tofu look more "egg-like," but also adds anti-inflammatory properties to this dish.

4. To build the burritos, place a tortilla on a plate or flat, clean surface. Add a generous dollop of hummus onto one half of the tortilla, leaving a border around the edges. Spoon some of the tofu scramble on top. Add some spinach, red bell pepper slices, tomato slices, shredded carrots, and a few slices of avocado. Fold in the sides of the tortilla over the filling and roll, tucking in the edges as you go. Repeat with the remaining tortillas and fillings.

5. Place a nonstick pan over medium heat. When the pan is hot, add the burritos seam side down. Cook covered until the bottoms of the burritos are lightly golden, about 3 minutes. Flip the burritos over and continue cooking for 2 to 3 more minutes or until lightly golden.

6. Remove from the pan, serve, and enjoy!

Almuerzo y Cena
(Lunch and Dinner)

Arroz con Gandules
(Rice with Pigeon Peas)

MAKES: 4–6 SERVINGS | PREP TIME: 15 MINUTES | COOKING TIME: 25 MINUTES

If there's any traditional dish that is quintessentially Puerto Rican, this is it. A must-have for every holiday and special event (and sometimes on a random Wednesday just because I'm craving it), it reminds me of home and family. Made with sofrito-infused basmati rice and pigeon peas, this recipe has all the flavors that are familiar, delicious, and comforting. This dish is typically made with pork or ham and served with a side of meat, so I was excited to put my own spin on it and make it 100 percent plant-based. Pigeon peas offer a good amount of iron and selenium and can even help prevent anemia, which is important when you're going plant-based.

INGREDIENTS

2 tablespoons olive oil

3 tablespoons Homemade Puerto Rican Sofrito (page 21)

3 tablespoons tomato sauce

2 cups basmati rice, rinsed

1 (15-ounce) can gandules (pigeon peas), drained and liquid reserved

12–15 Spanish olives

1½ cups water

Salt to taste

In our family, we cover the rice with a banana leaf to infuse it with a traditional flavor.

INSTRUCTIONS

1. Heat the olive oil in a pot over medium heat. Add the sofrito and tomato sauce and sauté for 2 to 3 minutes.

2. Add the rice and combine. Let the rice toast for 2 to 3 minutes or until just beginning to brown, stirring occasionally.

3. Add the gandules, olives, water, and the reserved liquid from the can of gandules and combine.

4. Season with salt to your liking and bring to a boil. Once boiling, reduce the heat to a simmer, cover, and let cook for 20 minutes.

5. Once ready, remove from the heat and fluff with a fork. Serve and enjoy!

Arroz Congrí
(Black Bean Rice)

MAKES: 4–6 SERVINGS | PREP TIME: 15 MINUTES | COOKING TIME: 25 MINUTES

When you want to make a plant-based meal for guests that's hearty, flavorful, and only uses one pot, this is my go-to recipe. It's a classic Cuban dish that's simmered in a delicious blend of herbs and spices and is typically served with Yuca con Mojo (page 115). I skipped the pork here in this flipped version of the traditional dish, but it still has all the rich, familiar flavors that make it one of my longtime favorites. If you love black beans, you are in luck—they are so good for you! One cup of them offers sixteen grams of plant protein and fifteen grams of fiber, which aids digestion and helps you stay fuller longer.

INGREDIENTS

2 tablespoons olive oil

1 medium yellow onion, chopped

1 green bell pepper, chopped and seeds removed

2 cloves garlic, minced

2 teaspoons ground cumin

1 teaspoon dried oregano

1 dried bay leaf

2 cups basmati rice, rinsed

2 cups cooked black beans, drained and liquid reserved

1 cup water

½ teaspoon salt

½ teaspoon ground pepper

To Serve

Mushroom Ropa Vieja (page 91)

INSTRUCTIONS

1. Heat the olive oil in a pot over medium heat. Once hot, add the onion and green bell pepper and sauté until soft and translucent, about 3 to 5 minutes. Add the garlic and combine.

2. Add the cumin, oregano, bay leaf, and rice and stir to combine.

3. Add the drained beans along with the reserved liquid and 1 cup water to the pot. Add salt and pepper and taste. The broth should be flavorful.

4. Bring the rice to a boil uncovered, then lower the heat to a simmer, cover tightly, and cook for 20 minutes.

5. Once done, fluff the rice with a fork, serve with Mushroom Ropa Vieja or your favorite side and enjoy!

Arroz Verde
(Green Rice)

MAKES: 4–6 SERVINGS | PREP TIME: 15 MINUTES | COOKING TIME: 25 MINUTES

I learned to make this recipe from my dad's partner, who is Dominican. I've also noticed it on menus at Mexican restaurants, which is just a reminder of how much culinary crossover there is among Latin cultures. Naturally plant-based, green rice is a great way to use up any herbs and leafy greens in your fridge. There are many ways to make it, but it always has a brightness and earthiness from the fresh green ingredients. I encourage you to serve this recipe however you like. Personally, I love it served with a side of black beans for an extra bit of protein.

INGREDIENTS

1 cup Swiss chard, chopped and stems removed

1 cup spinach leaves, chopped

1 cup parsley, chopped, plus more for serving

½ cup cilantro, chopped, plus more for serving

½ cup olive oil

3 cloves garlic

2 cups basmati rice, rinsed

2 cups boiling water

1 teaspoon salt

To Serve

½ cup cooked green peas

¼ cup green onion, chopped

INSTRUCTIONS

1. Add the Swiss chard, spinach leaves, parsley, cilantro, olive oil, and garlic into a food processor and process on high until it reaches a paste-like consistency.

2. Place a medium pot over medium-high heat. Once hot, transfer the green mixture to the pan and sauté until fragrant for 2 to 3 minutes.

3. Add the rice and mix to combine, coating the rice with the green mixture. Add in the boiling water and combine. Add the salt and let the rice come to a boil. Once boiling, reduce the heat to a simmer, cover, and cook for 20 minutes or until the rice is tender.

4. Once done, remove from the heat and use a fork to fluff the rice. Add the cooked green peas and green onion and combine.

5. Serve with more cilantro and parsley.

Chayote Salad

MAKES: 2–4 SERVINGS | PREP TIME: 15 MINUTES | COOKING TIME: 20 MINUTES

Originally from Mexico but grown around the world, chayote squash is actually a fruit. Because of its mild, versatile flavor, it's prepared like a vegetable. For those who have never tried it, I describe it as a cross between a cucumber and a potato. It's crisp but starchy and a little bit sweet and it's packed with vitamins B and C and potassium. Bonus: it's antimicrobial, which helps protect the digestive system and detox the liver. This is my Mami Abuelita's recipe. She'd prepare it in place of a traditional lettuce and tomato salad. I have vivid memories of her serving this often in a big white Pyrex® dish, which now would be a cool vintage piece of dishware. I wish I had it now to remind me of the moments we shared.

INGREDIENTS

2 chayotes, peeled, pitted, and cut into cubes

¼ cup olive oil

1 clove garlic, minced

Juice of 1 lime

1 cup frozen mixed vegetables (corn, green beans, peas, and carrots), thawed

½ cup red onion, chopped

Salt and pepper to taste

Fun fact: Some people in Latin American countries make similar versions of this with nopales, the pads from the Opuntia cacti.

INSTRUCTIONS

1. Place the chayote cubes in a pot and cover with water. Cook on medium heat for 15 to 20 minutes or until tender. Once tender, drain the water and set the chayote aside to cool.

2. In a large mixing bowl, add the olive oil, garlic, and lime juice and whisk to combine.

3. To the same mixing bowl, add the cooled chayote, mixed vegetables, and red onion and toss to combine.

4. Season with salt and pepper and serve.

Cuban-Style Lentil Picadillo

MAKES: 4–6 SERVINGS | PREP TIME: 15 MINUTES | COOKING TIME: 25 MINUTES

Picadillo, which literally translates to "chopped meat," is replaced by lentils in this traditional Cuban recipe. This one really takes me back to my childhood. My mom learned to make this from my stepfather's mom, who was Cuban, when we first moved to Miami. Typically, the potatoes are fried first and set aside to cool while the rest of the recipe is made. As kids, my brother and I would sneak into the kitchen to snack on the cooling potatoes every time my mom made this. When she caught on, she started making extra potatoes so the recipe wouldn't suffer!

In our house, we were definitely "team raisins." It's a hot debate among Latin families whether *picadillo* is authentic if it doesn't have raisins—some families are *firmly* anti-raisin. I love the added fiber of the raisins and the slightly sweet taste, but I'll leave it up to you to tweak this recipe however you like.

INGREDIENTS

Potatoes

1 cup olive oil

1 medium russet potato, peeled and cut into ½-inch cubes

Cuban-Style Picadillo

2 tablespoons olive oil

1 medium yellow onion, finely chopped

½ red bell pepper, finely chopped and seeds removed

2 cloves garlic, minced

1 teaspoon dried oregano

½ teaspoon ground cumin

½ teaspoon salt

¼ teaspoon ground black pepper

2 cups cooked lentils

¼ cup dry white wine

1 cup tomato sauce

¾ cup water

¼ cup Spanish olives, roughly chopped

2 dried bay leaves

¼ cup raisins, roughly chopped (optional)

To Serve

Cooked rice

Frituritas de Platano (page 45)

INSTRUCTIONS

1. To fry the potatoes, heat 1 cup olive oil in a frying pan over medium-high heat. Once hot, add the potatoes and fry for 5 to 6 minutes or until the potatoes are golden brown. Once ready, remove from oil and place on a plate lined with a paper towel to absorb excess oil and set them aside.

2. To make the picadillo, heat 2 tablespoons olive oil in a large pan over medium heat. Add the onions and cook until soft, about 3 to 5 minutes. Add the red bell pepper and garlic and cook for 1 to 2 more minutes.

3. Add in oregano, cumin, salt, and pepper, then add the cooked lentils and white wine and combine. Cook until the wine reduces a bit, about 2 to 3 minutes.

4. Add the tomato sauce, water, olives, and bay leaves and combine. Taste and adjust the seasoning if needed. Reduce the heat to medium-low, cover, and let cook, stirring occasionally for 3 to 5 minutes.

5. Add in the raisins and fried potatoes and combine. Cook for 1 to 2 more minutes to allow the sweetness of the raisins to infuse the lentil picadillo.

6. Once ready, remove from heat. Serve immediately with rice and Frituritas de Platano.

Cumin Rice

MAKES: 4–6 SERVINGS | PREP TIME: 10 MINUTES | COOKING TIME: 25 MINUTES

If you are anything like me, you can have rice all day, every day. I always crave it. This recipe uses basmati rice and is inspired by a recipe in an Ayurvedic cookbook that both my aunt Tata and my dad have on their bookshelves, but we modified it. Basmati rice is gluten-free and low in fat. It also has a low to medium glycemic index, which just means the carbohydrates in the rice are digested at a slower, steadier rate. This balances your overall energy levels. *Comino*, or cumin, is a spice with powerful properties, which our ancestors must've known, as it's used in so many Latin dishes (including sazón!). It helps ease irritable bowel syndrome. This recipe calls for cumin seeds, which you can also use to make a tea that reduces bloating. It's like a two-for-one deal.

INGREDIENTS

2 tablespoons olive oil

½ small yellow onion, chopped

2 tablespoons cumin seeds

½ teaspoon turmeric

¼ teaspoon ground black pepper

2 cups basmati rice, rinsed

2½ cups water

½ teaspoon salt

INSTRUCTIONS

1. Heat the olive oil in a pot over medium heat. Add the onion and sauté for 2 to 3 minutes or until soft and translucent.

2. Add in cumin seeds and toast for 1 to 2 minutes.

3. Add the turmeric and black pepper and combine. Cook 1 more minute to allow the spices to come together and release their flavors.

4. Add the rice and combine. Toast the rice for 1 to 2 minutes, stirring frequently.

5. Add the water and salt and mix. Bring the rice to a quick boil, reduce the heat to a simmer, and cover. Let cook for 15 to 20 minutes or until the water has evaporated and the rice is cooked through.

6. Once ready, uncover and fluff using a fork. Serve and enjoy!

Ayurvedic cooking was developed in India thousands of years ago and uses the philosophy that meals should be balanced according to nutritional properties and a person's unique constitution. If you're interested in the benefits of Ayurvedic cooking, I encourage you to learn more about it—it's really interesting and people have relied on it for thousands of years to stay aligned.

Eggplant Parm
with Tofu Ricotta "Cheese"

MAKES: 4–6 SERVINGS | PREP TIME: 20 MINUTES | COOKING TIME: 35 MINUTES

Attention eggplant parmesan lovers: If you thought going plant-based meant you'd be saying goodbye to this rich and delicious dish, think again. My husband and I worked together to "flip" this family favorite into a completely plant-based version. Instead of eggs, you'll dunk the eggplant into unsweetened dairy-free milk—*uns*weetened being the key detail here. You do not want your eggplant parm tasting like vanilla almond milk! Instead of frying the eggplant, this recipe is baked as a healthier alternative. For that reason, it calls for Panko breadcrumbs, which are just a little crispier, but regular ones work just fine, too. Eggplant is packed with vitamins A and C, which protect against cell damage, and the tomatoes in Joe's Marinara Sauce (page 26) are a great source of potassium, folate, and vitamin K.

INGREDIENTS

1½ cup unsweetened, unflavored
   dairy-free milk

2 cups Panko breadcrumbs

¼ cup nutritional yeast

2 teaspoons garlic powder

2 teaspoons Italian seasoning

2 medium eggplants, peeled and cut
   lengthwise into ¼-inch slices

2–3 cups Joe's Marinara Sauce (page 26),
   divided

2 cups Tofu Ricotta "Cheese" (page 31),
   divided

To Serve

⅓ cup fresh basil, chopped

INSTRUCTIONS

1. Preheat the oven to 375°F. Line 1 to 2 baking sheets with parchment paper and set them aside.

2. Set aside 2 mixing bowls. In one bowl add dairy-free milk and in the other bowl add Panko, nutritional yeast, garlic powder, and Italian seasoning and combine.

3. Dip the eggplant slices one at a time into the dairy-free milk, then into the breadcrumbs, and place onto the baking sheet. Repeat this process until all the eggplant slices are well coated in the breadcrumbs.

4. Spray the slices with cooking spray and bake for 15 to 20 minutes or until the eggplant is tender and the breadcrumbs are golden brown. Once ready, remove from the oven and set aside.

5. To assemble the eggplant parm, pour ½ cup of Joe's Marinara Sauce into a 9 x 9-inch baking dish (or similar sized baking dish). Add a layer of cooked eggplant, top it with more sauce and scoops of the Tofu Ricotta "Cheese," and repeat this process until all fillings and eggplant slices are used up.

6. Place the eggplant parm in the oven to bake for 15 minutes. Remove from the oven, top with fresh basil, and enjoy!

Garbanzos Guisados
(Chickpea Stew)

MAKES: 4–6 SERVINGS | PREP TIME: 15 MINUTES | COOKING TIME: 20 MINUTES

When I was a kid, my mom would make this comforting stew all the time. I'd catch a glimpse of her draining the chickpeas, then sneak into the kitchen to grab a taste of the golden salsita or what I called "the little sauce," the broth of the stew. "Karla!" she'd exclaim, shooing me out of the kitchen. "Salte de ahi!" Whether I ate it by itself or drizzled it over white rice, that stew always tasted like comfort. It wasn't until later that I learned that chickpeas were loaded with great stuff like magnesium, zinc, and fiber. Sometimes kids *do* know what's good for them!

INGREDIENTS

1 tablespoon olive oil

2 tablespoons Homemade Puerto Rican Sofrito (page 21)

1 tablespoon Homemade Adobo (page 18)

½ tablespoon Homemade Sazón (page 24)

½ cup tomato sauce

1 (16-ounce) can chickpeas, drained and rinsed

1 cup potatoes, cut into small cubes

1 medium carrot, cut into small cubes

1 cup calabaza squash, cut into small cubes and seeds removed

3 cups water

1 dried bay leaf

½ teaspoon salt

½ teaspoon ground black pepper

½ cup fresh cilantro, chopped

To Serve

Cooked rice

Sliced avocado

INSTRUCTIONS

1. Heat the olive oil in a pot over medium heat. Add sofrito, adobo, and sazón and sauté for 2–3 minutes.

2. Add the tomato sauce, chickpeas, potatoes, carrots, and calabaza squash and combine.

3. Add the water, bay leaf, salt, and pepper and mix to combine.

4. Let cook until the stew comes to a boil, then reduce the heat to a simmer, cover, and let cook for 12 to 15 minutes more or until the vegetables are tender.

5. Once the vegetables are tender, shut off the heat, add fresh cilantro, and combine.

6. Serve with a scoop of rice and slices of fresh avocado and enjoy!

Grilled Cauliflower Steaks
with Cilantro Chimichurri

MAKES: 4–6 SERVINGS | PREP TIME: 15 MINUTES | COOKING TIME: 15 MINUTES

This is my go-to recipe for grilling in the summer. My husband throws these cauliflower "steaks" on the grill, and they are ready in just a few minutes! Cauliflower is loaded with fiber and antioxidants that help with inflammation, which makes this recipe both filling and great for the gut. I tell my clients all the time that good health starts with a healthy gut (they are probably sick of hearing it!), but it's true: The more you eat the rainbow—fruits and veggies of all different colors—the better. If you get bored of cauliflower easily, switch up the ingredients to suit your cravings. I pair it with chimichurri because I love the refreshing cilantro taste in the summer, but I also love it baked with a slice of plant-based cheese and Joe's Marinara Sauce (page 26). Have fun with it!

INGREDIENTS

⅓ cup olive oil

1–2 clove(s) garlic, minced

½ teaspoon dried oregano

½ teaspoon salt

½ teaspoon ground black pepper

2 heads cauliflower, leaves removed and cut into 1-inch steaks

To Serve
Cilantro Chimichurri (page 13)

INSTRUCTIONS

1. Turn the grill on high heat.

2. In a mixing bowl, add the olive oil, minced garlic, oregano, salt, and pepper and whisk to combine.

3. Brush the olive oil mixture on both sides of each cauliflower steak and place on the grill to cook for 2 to 3 minutes or until cauliflower steaks show grill marks on each side.

4. Lower the heat to medium and continue to cook covered for 4 to 5 minutes or until the cauliflower steaks are tender.

5. While the cauliflower steaks are on the grill, prepare the Cilantro Chimichurri.

6. Once the cauliflower steaks are ready, remove from the grill and place on a serving dish. Spread a generous amount of chimichurri over the cauliflower steaks, serve, and enjoy!

Guineitos en Escabeche
(Pickled Green Banana Salad)

MAKES: 9–10 SERVINGS | PREP TIME: 15 MINUTES | COOKING TIME: 25 MINUTES

This salty, tangy dish is super popular in Puerto Rico. It's also very versatile. Some people use yucca instead of unripe bananas, but bananas are loaded with prebiotics, probiotics, and fiber, which are all great for your gut. Traditionally, this recipe is made with white vinegar, but I think apple cider vinegar is a nice upgrade. Apple cider vinegar aids healthy digestion and may improve insulin sensitivity and help lower blood sugar after meals.

INGREDIENTS

8 green bananas, peeled and cut into 1-inch rounds

1 teaspoon salt

1 cup olive oil

1 medium red or yellow onion, thinly sliced

2 cloves garlic, minced

2 dried bay leaves

12 black peppercorns

½ cup apple cider vinegar

15 whole Spanish olives

Salt and pepper to taste

To Serve

Sliced avocado

Fresh cilantro, chopped, to garnish

INSTRUCTIONS

1. To a large pot, add the green bananas, cover with water, and add the salt. Turn the heat to medium-high and bring to a boil. Once boiling, reduce the heat to medium and let cook for 15 minutes or until tender (but not too tender that they break apart).

2. While the green bananas cook, place a saucepan over medium-low heat. Add the olive oil, onion, garlic, bay leaves, and peppercorns and continue cooking on medium-low heat for 5 to 7 minutes (you don't want the onions or garlic to brown, just soften). Once ready, shut off the heat, add in the apple cider vinegar, and combine.

If you can't find green bananas at the grocery store, you can use green plantains. Just adjust the measurements in the recipe, as plantains are larger.

3. Drain the cooked green bananas and transfer to a large mixing bowl to allow them to cool. Once cooled, add in the escabeche mixture and olives and mix to combine. Taste and adjust the seasoning by adding more salt and pepper if needed.

4. Cover and allow to marinate for 4 hours or overnight. Serve cold or at room temperature with sliced avocado and fresh cilantro.

Habichuelas Guisadas
(Red Kidney Bean Stew)

MAKES: 4–6 SERVINGS | PREP TIME: 15 MINUTES | COOKING TIME: 20 MINUTES

My abuelo didn't consider dinner a proper dinner unless it included stewed kidney beans, white rice, and some kind of meat. If Abuela served soup he'd say "Who's sick? Where's the rice and beans?" I can hear him right now and smell these beans simmering on the stove. Beans have always been a staple in Latin cooking because of their low cost and high protein. In moments throughout history, Latin communities have relied on beans for their health benefits during times of political and economic crisis. I always keep several cans on hand so I can boost any dish with more protein. This popular, savory dish is native to Puerto Rico and packed with flavorful, clean ingredients. It features kidney beans simmered in sofrito, tomato sauce, olives, potatoes, and calabaza squash and it's typically served with white rice. Personally, I love it alongside basmati rice and topped with sliced avocado.

INGREDIENTS

1 tablespoon olive oil

2 tablespoons Homemade Puerto Rican Sofrito (page 21)

1 tablespoon Homemade Adobo (page 18)

½ tablespoon Homemade Sazón (page 24)

½ cup tomato sauce

1 (16-ounce) can red kidney beans, drained and rinsed

1 cup potatoes, cut into small cubes

1 cup calabaza squash, cut into small cubes and seeds removed

2 cups water

½ teaspoon salt

½ teaspoon ground black pepper

To Serve

Cooked rice

Sliced avocado

INSTRUCTIONS

1. Heat the olive oil in a pot over medium heat. Add the sofrito, adobo, and sazón and sauté for 2 to 3 minutes.

2. Add the tomato sauce, beans, potatoes, and squash and combine.

3. Add in the water, salt, and pepper and stir to mix. Taste and adjust the seasoning if needed.

4. Bring the beans to bring to a boil. Once boiling, reduce the heat to a simmer, cover, and let cook for 12 to 15 minutes or until the vegetables are tender.

5. Serve with rice and sliced avocado and enjoy!

Loaded Sweet Potato Nachos
with Cilantro Dressing

MAKES: 2–4 SERVINGS | PREP TIME: 15 MINUTES | COOKING TIME: 30 MINUTES

Sometimes I get super creative in the kitchen with my husband, and this recipe is the perfect example. We love nachos (who doesn't?) so we wanted to replicate a healthier version without the cheese or the chips. Thin-sliced sweet potatoes make a sturdy chip when you roast them in the oven—plus, they have so much more fiber. After you prep your chips, you can add any toppings you like. We love black beans, corn, avocado, and jalapeños (at a minimum) but feel free to add anything your heart desires.

INGREDIENTS

Sweet Potato "Chips"

2 medium size sweet potatoes, peeled

1–2 tablespoons olive oil

½ teaspoon salt

½ teaspoon ground black pepper

Toppings

1 (15-ounce) can black beans, drained and
   rinsed

1 cup sweet corn

1 cup tomatoes, chopped

¼ cup red onion, chopped

2 tablespoons fresh lime juice

1½ teaspoons salt

½ jalapeño, chopped and seeds removed
   (optional)

To Serve

1 avocado, pit removed, peeled, and
   chopped

¼–½ cup Cilantro Dressing (page 14)

¼ cup fresh cilantro, chopped

INSTRUCTIONS

1. Preheat the oven to 400°F. Line 1 to 2 baking sheets with parchment paper and set aside.

2. Using a mandolin slicer or knife, slice the sweet potatoes into ¼-inch thick slices.

3. Transfer the sweet potato slices to a large mixing bowl. Add olive oil, salt, and pepper and toss to combine. Lay the slices in an even layer on the baking sheet(s) and bake for 25 to 30 minutes or until crisp. Once ready, remove from the oven and set aside.

4. To make the toppings, add black beans, corn, tomatoes, red onion, lime juice, salt, and jalapeño (if using) to a mixing bowl and combine. Taste and adjust the seasoning if needed.

5. To serve, arrange the sweet potato chips on a large platter and add toppings of choice along with chopped avocado, Cilantro Dressing, and cilantro. Enjoy!

Mushroom Ropa Vieja

MAKES: 2–4 SERVINGS | PREP TIME: 20 MINUTES | COOKING TIME: 35 MINUTES

Splitting time between Miami and Puerto Rico, some of the dishes we had in Miami were heavily influenced by traditionally Cuban cuisine. You might notice that Cuban, Puerto Rican, and Dominican dishes have a lot of similarities. My mom was always picking up culinary tips from my stepfather, integrating techniques and ingredients from his cultural dishes into her Puerto Rican dishes. It's this beautiful mashup that makes family recipes so special, I think.

Ropa vieja is the ultimate Cuban dish. It's traditionally made with beef, but my version swaps out the beef for king oyster mushrooms, which have a similar fibrous texture and absorb the heavily aromatic sauce so perfectly. Mushrooms also encourage blood sugar control and provide antioxidant and anti-inflammatory benefits. There's so much to love with this updated fan favorite. Enjoy!

INGREDIENTS

4–5 king oyster mushrooms

3 tablespoons olive oil, divided

½ medium yellow onion, chopped

½ red bell pepper, cut into strips and seeds removed

½ green bell pepper, cut into strips and seeds removed

½ yellow bell pepper, cut into strips and seeds removed

2 cloves garlic, minced

1 teaspoon dried oregano

1 teaspoon ground cumin

1 dried bay leaf

½ cup tomato sauce

½ cup white wine

6–10 Spanish olives

1 tablespoon capers

¼ teaspoon salt

¼ teaspoon ground black pepper

To Serve

Arroz Congri (page 69)

Frituritas de Platano (page 45)

(Continued)

INSTRUCTIONS

1. Preheat the oven to 400°F. Line a baking sheet with parchment paper and set it aside.

2. Using a damp paper towel, clean the mushrooms. Using two forks, shred the mushroom stems and caps into long pieces.

3. Set the shredded mushrooms on the lined baking dish, drizzle with 1 tablespoon olive oil, and roast for 15 to 20 minutes or until the edges start to crisp. Remove from oven and set aside.

4. Heat the remaining olive oil in a pan over medium heat. Add the onion and peppers and let cook until caramelized, about 10 to 12 minutes.

5. Add the garlic, oregano, cumin, bay leaf, tomato sauce, and wine and combine. Add in the cooked mushrooms and mix well. Let cook for 3 to 5 minutes or until all the flavors are well incorporated.

6. Add the olives, capers, salt, and pepper and mix. Taste and adjust the seasoning if needed.

7. Serve with Arroz Congri and Frituritas de Platano. Enjoy!

Pastelón
(Puerto Rican Sweet Plantain Lasagna)

MAKES: 4–6 SERVINGS | PREP TIME: 15 MINUTES | COOKING TIME: 30 MINUTES

Plátanos maduros are the star players here and take the place of lasagna sheets in this veggie-rich lasagna. Sometimes referred to as *piñon,* this dish was one of my mom's go-tos. The naturally sweet flavor of bright yellow, ripe plantains caramelized in the frying pan paired with the saltiness of the veggies is so nostalgic for me. Traditionally, pastelón is made with ground beef and a lot of cheese and egg but this flipped version plays on the warm layers of plantains with a healthy dose of tender carrots and mixed vegetables standing in for the beef, cheese, and egg. Plantains have a long history in Caribbean culinary traditions and are woven into Puerto Rican culture. They also have incredible health benefits, including vitamin A, which helps with cell regeneration (hello, gorgeous skin!), and potassium. Introduce this take on the classic dish to your family with a colorful Kale Salad (page 49). It'll be a crowd-pleaser.

INGREDIENTS

¾ cup olive oil

4–5 ripe plantains (the skins should be yellow and black), peeled, sliced lengthwise

2 tablespoons Homemade Puerto Rican Sofrito (page 21)

½ cup tomato sauce

½ yellow onion, chopped

1 Italian green pepper (friarelli), chopped and seeds removed

1 (16-ounce) package frozen mixed vegetables (corn, green beans, peas, and carrots)

1 tablespoon Homemade Adobo (page 18)

½ tablespoons Homemade Sazón (page 24)

½ teaspoon salt

¼ teaspoon ground black pepper

1 cup shredded dairy-free cheddar cheese (optional)

INSTRUCTIONS

1. Preheat the oven to 350°F.

2. Heat the olive oil in a large skillet over medium-high heat. Add the plantain slices and fry for 1 to 2 minutes or until they turn a golden honey color. Once ready, transfer the cooked plantains to a plate lined with a paper towel to drain the excess oil and set aside.

3. Place another large skillet over medium heat, add the sofrito and tomato sauce, and sauté for 1 to 2 minutes. Add the onion and pepper and sauté for 3 to 5 minutes or until tender. Add a small amount of water if needed to avoid browning.

(Continued)

4. Add the frozen vegetables, adobo, sazón, salt, and pepper and combine. Taste and adjust the seasoning if needed. Cover and let cook until the vegetables are heated through and tender.

5. Add dairy-free cheese and mix. Continue to cook for 1 to 2 more minutes or until the cheese has melted. Shut off the heat and set it aside.

6. To build the pastelón, lightly grease a 9 x-9-inch oven-safe casserole dish with nonstick cooking spray. Place half of the plantain slices on the bottom of the dish, then evenly distribute the vegetable mixture on top, making sure to spread the mixture to the edges of the dish. Top with the remaining plantain slices.

7. Place the dish in the oven and bake for 15 to 20 minutes or until the edges start to turn golden brown. Once ready, remove from the oven and let cool slightly before serving.

Sancocho
(Root Vegetable Stew)

MAKES: 4–6 SERVINGS | PREP TIME: 15 MINUTES | COOKING TIME: 40 MINUTES

If you're Latin, you've probably had *sancocho* for a special occasion. This stew is chock-full of spices, aromatics, and veggies, so it takes time to make. I think of it like a "love note" from whoever is making it. When Abuela would make it, she'd call my mom in the middle of the day to give her a heads-up. She knew it was the kind of surprise that would make her day. They would enjoy a big bowl for lunch and catch up. To me, this stew is about family, togetherness, and comfort. *Yautia* is a thinner root vegetable that is completely white inside and *malanga* is a thicker root vegetable that is also white but with tiny purple specs. Malanga is a great source of potassium, which can help regulate blood pressure and reduce muscle cramps.

INGREDIENTS

2 tablespoons olive oil

2 tablespoons Homemade Puerto Rican Sofrito (page 21)

1 cup yellow split peas

2 cups water

6 cups Caldo de Vegetables (page 10)

¼ pound yuca, peeled and cut into medium-sized pieces

¼ pound yautia, peeled and cut into medium-sized pieces

¼ pound malanga, peeled and cut into medium-sized pieces

¼ pound calabaza squash, peeled and cut into medium-sized pieces

1 green plantain, peeled and cut into ½-inch rounds

1 corn on the cob, cut into 1-inch rounds

1 teaspoon ground turmeric

1 teaspoon salt

¼ teaspoon ground black pepper

½ cup fresh cilantro, chopped

½ cup fresh parsley, chopped

To Serve

Cooked rice

Sliced avocado

Sancocho has been enjoyed by people all over the world. It originated in Africa and was later adapted in countries like Puerto Rico, Columbia, the Dominican Republic, Venezuela, and Cuba.

(Continued)

INSTRUCTIONS

1. Heat the olive oil in a large pot over medium heat. Add sofrito and sauté for 1 to 2 minutes. Add in the split peas and coat evenly with the sofrito.

2. Add the water and combine. Reduce the heat to low, cover, and let cook for 10 to 12 minutes or until the split peas are tender. Add more water if needed to maintain the same level of liquid and stir occasionally.

3. Once the split peas are tender, add Caldo de Vegetables, yuca, yautia, malanga, squash, plantain, and corn and combine.

4. Add turmeric, salt, and pepper and mix. Taste and adjust the seasoning if needed. Bring the heat to medium and continue to cook the stew for 20 to 25 minutes or until the vegetables and roots are cooked through.

5. Once ready, shut off the heat. Add the cilantro and parsley and combine.

6. Serve with a scoop of cooked rice and sliced avocado.

Scalloped Potatoes

MAKES 4–6 SERVINGS | PREP TIME: 15 MINUTES | COOKING TIME: 55 MINUTES

I have vivid memories of boxed scalloped potatoes, as I think every eighties and nineties kid who spent time in North America does. Convenience cooking was big during that time since so many parents were working outside of the home. My mom used to call me from work asking that I start dinner and at least once a week boxed scalloped potatoes were on the menu. I still remember the papery freeze-dried potatoes and the dry cheese mix I'd blend with milk. Funny how some memories around food just stick with you. I actually loved scalloped potato night and wanted to create a recipe that was easy and mimicked the flavors I remember from the boxed version of my childhood, but without all the preservatives, so my version uses dairy-free milk, skips the cheese, and uses a combo of sweet potatoes and white potatoes. Sweet potatoes come in several colors and sizes and they're high in fiber, vitamins, and minerals. Plus, they feed the good bacteria in your gut. For a little color and savory finish, these potatoes are topped with fresh scallions. *Way* better than the box.

INGREDIENTS

2–3 medium size Yukon gold potatoes, washed

3 tablespoons vegan butter or olive oil

1 small yellow onion, diced

2 cloves garlic, minced

3 tablespoons all-purpose flour

3 cups unflavored, unsweetened dairy-free milk

½ teaspoon salt

¼ teaspoon ground black pepper

To Serve

¼ cup scallions, chopped

INSTRUCTIONS

1. Preheat oven to 400°F.

2. Using a mandolin slicer or knife, slice the potatoes into ¼-inch-thick slices, then place them in a large bowl of water to prevent them from turning brown. Set them aside.

3. Heat the butter or oil in a large pan or skillet over medium heat. Add the onion and sauté for 3 to 5 minutes or until soft. Add the garlic and sauté for 1 to 2 more minutes.

(Continued)

4. Add the flour and mix until a paste forms and coats the onion. Slowly add the dairy-free milk and whisk to combine until the flour lumps dissolve and the sauce is smooth.

5. Raise the heat to high and bring the mixture to a boil, stirring frequently. Once boiling, reduce the heat to a simmer and continue stirring frequently for 5 minutes or until the mixture starts to thicken. Once ready, add the salt and pepper and combine. Taste and adjust the seasoning if needed.

6. Pour some of the mixture into the bottom of a 10-inch baking or casserole dish. Layer the potatoes and top with more mixture. Repeat until all of the potatoes and mixture are used.

7. Place the dish in the oven to bake for 30 to 40 minutes or until the potatoes are fork tender and top is lightly browned.

8. Once ready, remove from the oven and garnish with scallions.

Sopa de Calabaza
(Calabaza Squash Soup)

MAKES: 4–6 SERVINGS | PREP TIME: 15 MINUTES | COOKING TIME: 30 MINUTES

As my aunt Tata would say, "Esto se hace en un momento!" or "This soup is ready in a minute!" It's also super filling and nutritious, thanks to the calabaza squash, a great source of vitamins A, B, C, thiamine, riboflavin, and beta-carotene. Fun fact: Calabaza is the generic name in Spanish for any type of pumpkin. In an English-language context it refers to what's best known as West Indian pumpkin and in Latin dishes we use it in beans, rice, and, of course, Sancocho (page 97).

That said, if you can't find it, you can sub in regular pumpkin, butternut squash, or acorn squash to make this recipe. Just make sure you aren't using a squash or pumpkin that's too sweet. The consistency of the blended calabaza makes this soup super creamy and thick, but it's 100 percent dairy-free (and you'd never know it).

INGREDIENTS

5–6 cups (about 2 pounds) calabaza squash, peeled, cubed, and seeds removed

½ yellow onion

1 green bell pepper, seeds removed

2 cloves garlic, peeled

5 cups Caldo de Vegetables (page 10) or water

¼ cup fresh cilantro, chopped

¼ cup fresh parsley, chopped

½ teaspoon salt

½ teaspoon ground black pepper

To Serve

Toasted pumpkin seeds

Red pepper flakes (optional)

INSTRUCTIONS

1. Place a large pot over medium heat. Add squash, onion, green bell pepper, garlic, and Caldo de Vegetables and combine. Bring to a boil, then reduce to a simmer and let cook for 20 to 30 minutes or until the vegetables are tender. Once tender, shut off the heat and let cool slightly.

2. Using a hand blender, blend the vegetables until smooth and creamy.

3. Once smooth, add cilantro, parsley, salt, and pepper and combine. Taste and adjust the seasoning if needed.

4. Serve with toasted pumpkin seeds and a sprinkle of red pepper flakes. Enjoy!

Sopa de Lentejas
(Lentil Soup)

MAKES: 4–6 SERVINGS | PREP TIME: 15 MINUTES | COOKING TIME: 25 MINUTES

This hearty, healthy soup is perfect for when you don't feel like cooking but want a healthy meal. During my busier weeks, I depend on this (plus, you can make a huge batch for leftovers because it freezes beautifully). It's a simple recipe, but it gives all the comforting feels and delicious flavor. I love tweaking it according to my mood and what I have in my fridge: I encourage you to do the same! When I'm craving more of a Latin-inspired soup, I'll add 1 tablespoon Homemade Adobo (page 18) and ½ tablespoon Homemade Sazón (page 24). If I'm craving more veggies, I'll throw whatever I have in the pot. One cup of lentils provides an impressive ninety percent of your recommended folic acid, plus they're packed with fiber and protein.

INGREDIENTS

1 tablespoon olive oil

1 small yellow onion, chopped

3 cloves garlic, minced

1 medium carrot, peeled and chopped

1 (14.5-ounce) can diced tomatoes

1 cup dry lentils, soaked at least 1 hour, rinsed, and drained

4–5 cups Caldo de Vegetables (page 10) or water

½ teaspoon ground turmeric

½ teaspoon salt

¼ teaspoon ground black pepper

¼–½ cup fresh cilantro, chopped (optional)

INSTRUCTIONS

1. Heat the olive oil in a pot over medium heat. Add the onions and sauté for 2 to 3 minutes. Add the garlic and cook for 1 to 2 more minutes.

2. Add the carrot, diced tomatoes, lentils, Caldo de Vegetables or water and combine. Add in turmeric, salt, and pepper and mix well. Taste and adjust the seasoning if needed.

3. Continue to cook the lentils on medium heat until they come to a boil. Once boiling, reduce the heat to a simmer. Cover and let cook, stirring occasionally, for 20 to 25 minutes or until the lentils and vegetables are tender.

4. Once ready, shut off the heat, add fresh cilantro, and stir to combine. Serve and enjoy!

If your digestion is sensitive to lentils, soak and rinse them well in cold water before cooking.

Sopa de Papa y Cilantro
(Creamy Cilantro and Potato Soup)

My aunt Tata taught me how to make this years ago, before I really knew my way around the kitchen. It's super easy to make and uses ingredients you probably have in your kitchen right now. Plus, it only takes twenty minutes. I like to make a big batch and freeze the leftovers for an easy grab-and-go meal for work or when I don't have the energy or time to whip up a dinner from scratch. The Caldo de Vegetables (page 10), cilantro, and black pepper are all anti-inflammatory and the pumpkin seeds are rich in iron, zinc, and antioxidants. I say feel free to add as much as you want for garnish! This soup is pretty much a warm hug in a bowl, so rely on this recipe when you need a little comfort.

INGREDIENTS

1 tablespoon olive oil

½ yellow onion, chopped

1 clove garlic, minced

3 medium size potatoes, peeled and cut into cubes

4 cups Caldo de Vegetables (page 10) or water

½ teaspoon ground turmeric

½ teaspoon salt

¼ teaspoon ground black pepper

1 bunch cilantro leaves, plus more for serving

Fun fact: Incas in Peru were the first to cultivate papas or potatoes between 8,000 BC and 4,000 BC.

INSTRUCTIONS

1. Heat the olive oil in a pot over medium heat. Add the onion and cook for 3 to 5 minutes until soft. Add the garlic and sauté for 1 to 2 more minutes.

2. Add the potatoes, Caldo de Vegetables or water, turmeric, salt, and pepper and combine. Bring to a boil, then reduce the heat to a simmer. Cook for 12 to 15 minutes or until the potatoes are tender.

3. Once the potatoes are tender, shut off the heat, add cilantro, cover the pot, and let sit for 1 to 2 minutes. The heat allows the cilantro to release its flavor without overcooking it.

4. Carefully transfer the soup to a blender and blend on high until smooth and creamy.

5. Serve with more cilantro.

Sopa de Platano
(Plantain Soup)

If you're Caribbean, you probably grew up having a lot of *sopa de platano*. I certainly did and I loved it. Infused with traditional flavors like cilantro, bell peppers, and garlic, it's a starchy, creamy soup that's naturally dairy-free and great for lunch or dinner. You can use your Homemade Puerto Rican Sofrito (page 21), Homemade Adobo (page 18), and Caldo de Vegetales (page 10) in this recipe. It's how Abuela would make it: just simple, high-quality ingredients and nothing extra. Cooked green plantains are the main ingredient here and taste a little less sweet than mature plantains, but they're still so delicious and super healthy, offering a dose of fiber and vitamins A and C. This recipe proves that traditional dishes from Caribbean culture have been plant-based for centuries (way before veganism was a trend, in fact!).

INGREDIENTS

2 tablespoons olive oil

2 tablespoons Homemade Puerto Rican
  Sofrito (page 21)

1 tablespoon Homemade Adobo (page 18)

½ tablespoon Homemade Sazón (page 24)

3 large green plantains, peeled and cut into
  ½-inch rounds

1 medium size carrot, peeled and cubed

1 celery rib, chopped

6 cups Caldo de Vegetales (page 10) or
  water

1 dried bay leaf

1 teaspoon salt

½ teaspoon ground black pepper

¼ cup fresh cilantro, chopped, plus more for
  serving

To Serve

Plantain chips

Lime wedges

INSTRUCTIONS

1. Heat the olive oil in a large pot over medium heat. Add sofrito, adobo, and sazón and sauté for 1 to 2 minutes.

2. Add the plantains, carrot, and celery and evenly coat with the sofrito mixture. Let cook for 1 to 2 more minutes. Add the Caldo de Vegetales or water, bay leaf, salt, and pepper and combine.

3. Raise the heat to high and bring the soup to a boil. Once boiling, lower the heat to a simmer, cover, and cook for 25 to 30 minutes or until the vegetables are tender.

4. Once the vegetables are tender, add the cilantro and combine. Shut off the heat and let cool slightly.

5. Using a hand blender or potato masher, puree the soup. Taste and adjust the seasoning if needed.

6. Serve with plantain chips, lime wedges, and more cilantro.

Sorullitos de Maíz
(Corn Fritters)

MAKES: 15–20 SORULLITOS | PREP TIME: 10 MINUTES | COOKING TIME: 20 MINUTES

My mom was super excited that I was including this recipe in my book because it was inspired by a recipe passed down from her mom. She remembers my abuela cooking this traditional Puerto Rican snack and enjoying the gooey, cheesy fritters as soon as they came out of the pan (waiting any longer ruins the experience!). This upgraded version uses dairy-free cheese and a touch of sugar for the perfect mix of sweet and savory. Corn gets a bad rap, because it has become so genetically modified, but naturally grown corn is really good for you. It's a great source of fiber and essential nutrients. Cornmeal, made from grinding corn kernels into a coarse powder, doesn't contain gluten either, so it's a safe ingredient (and sometimes even a flour substitute) for those with gluten intolerance and celiac disease. I'm a big fan of corn and a big fan of these fritters.

INGREDIENTS

2 cups water

1 tablespoon vegan butter

3 tablespoons brown sugar

1 teaspoon salt

1¼ cups yellow cornmeal (organic if possible)

½ cups dairy-free cheddar cheese, shredded

Olive oil for frying

To Serve

Mayo Ketchup (page 27)

INSTRUCTIONS

1. In a saucepan over medium heat, combine the water, butter, brown sugar, and salt. Bring to a boil, then slowly whisk in the cornmeal. Continue stirring for 3 to 5 minutes or until a soft ball is formed.

2. Remove from heat and let cool until able to handle. If the dough is crumbly, add warm water a little at a time. If the dough sticks to your fingers, add more cornmeal (a little sticky is good).

3. Take scoops of dough and knead between your fingers until smooth. Roll into a log approximately 1 inch wide and 3 inches long. Press down and stuff with dairy-free cheese, then smooth the dough so the cheese is covered. Repeat with the remaining dough.

4. Working in batches, fry the sorullitos in hot olive oil that is at least 2 inches deep. Cook for 3 to 4 minutes or until golden brown.

5. Once browned, remove from the oil and place on a plate lined with a paper towel to absorb the excess oil.

6. Serve with Mayo Ketchup or your favorite dipping sauce and enjoy.

Sweet Potato Shepherd's Pie

MAKES: 8–10 SERVINGS | PREP TIME: 15 MINUTES | COOKING TIME: 1 HOUR

Traditional shepherd's pie is made of minced meat, whipped potatoes, and cheese and it's super satisfying. This upgraded version is just as hearty but has rich, savory, plant-based ingredients. In place of meat, you'll use a sauteed mix of onion, bell peppers, and mushrooms along with lentils for a punch of protein. Lentils are an incredible meat substitute, thanks to their texture and flavor. And, because it's me, I add cilantro and Homemade Sazón (page 24) for a little Latin kick. Fun fact: You can feel great about eating sweet potatoes. Just one cup of baked sweet potato provides nearly half of your recommended vitamin C needs and 400 percent of your recommended vitamin A intake. Both of these nutrients support a strong immune system, which is even more important during cold and flu season. Make this your winter go-to dish!

INGREDIENTS

Sweet Potatoes

3 large sweet potatoes, washed, peeled, and cubed

2 tablespoons vegan butter or olive oil

1 teaspoon salt

½ teaspoon ground black pepper

Vegetable Filling

2 tablespoons olive oil

1 small yellow onion, chopped

½ green bell pepper, chopped and seeds removed

½ red bell pepper, chopped and seeds removed

2 cloves garlic, minced

1 teaspoon Homemade Sazón (page 24)

2½ cups shiitake mushrooms, sliced

2 cups crushed tomatoes

1½ cups brown lentils, soaked 1–2 hours, drained, and rinsed

4 cups water

1 (10-ounce) bag frozen mixed veggies (peas, carrots, green beans, and corn)

3 cups kale or spinach, chopped

¼ cup fresh cilantro, chopped, plus more for serving

½ teaspoon salt

½ teaspoon ground black pepper

INSTRUCTIONS

1. For the sweet potatoes, place a large pot over high heat. Add the sweet potatoes and cover with water. Bring to a boil, then reduce the heat to medium-high and cook for 15 to 20 minutes or until tender.

2. While the sweet potatoes are cooking, preheat the oven to 425°F and lightly grease a 9 × 13-inch (or similar size) baking dish. Set aside.

3. When the sweet potatoes are tender, drain the water and transfer to a large mixing bowl. Add 2 tablespoons butter or oil, salt, and pepper and use a potato masher or fork to mash until smooth. Once ready, cover and set aside.

4. For the vegetable filling, heat 2 tablespoons olive oil in a large pot over medium heat. Add the onion and peppers and sauté for 3 to 5 minutes or until they start to soften. Add the garlic and sazón and sauté for another 1 to 2 minutes. Add mushrooms, crushed tomatoes, lentils, and water and combine. Bring to a boil, then reduce the heat to a simmer. Continue cooking for 15 to 20 minutes or until lentils are tender. In the last 5 minutes of cooking the lentils, add the frozen veggies and kale or spinach and combine. Once all the vegetables are tender, add the cilantro, salt, and pepper and mix to combine. Taste and adjust the flavor if needed. Once ready, remove from heat.

5. Carefully transfer the lentil mixture to your baking dish and top with the mashed sweet potatoes, smoothing it out with a spoon. Bake for 15 minutes or until the edges start to brown.

6. Remove the dish from the oven and let cool slightly before serving. Once ready, top with more cilantro, serve, and enjoy!

Tofu "Bistec" en Salsa

MAKES: 2–4 SERVINGS | PREP TIME: 15 MINUTES | COOKING TIME: 15 MINUTES

I love all things soupy or "con salsita." There's just something so comforting about a flavorful stew or sauce poured over rice. In the case of the classic Latin and Caribbean dish *con bistec*, or with cube steak, the soupy tomato sauce is made with herbs and spices and served with rice and plantains. I replace the steak in the traditional dish with firm tofu and it does not disappoint!

Fun fact: If you want to boost the nutritional value of any dish, combining foods and spices is a great way to do it. For example, this recipe uses paste from tomatoes, a source of lycopene, which helps manage healthy levels of cholesterol. When tomatoes are sauteed in olive oil, it helps the body absorb lycopene easier. Other hacks, like combining pepper and turmeric, magnify each spice's anti-inflammatory properties. There are so many ways to combine your ingredients to enhance their natural benefits. I encourage you to do further reading to arm yourself with this awesome information as you continue your plant-based journey!

INGREDIENTS

1 tablespoon olive oil

2 tablespoon Homemade Puerto Rican Sofrito (page 21)

1 tablespoon Homemade Adobo (page 18)

½ tablespoon Homemade Sazón (page 24)

2 tablespoons tomato paste

1 yellow onion, sliced

1 clove garlic, minced

1 (8-ounce) can tomato sauce

½ cup water

½ teaspoon salt

¼ teaspoon ground black pepper

½ (14-ounce) block extra firm tofu, drained and cut into ½-inch thick slices

To Serve

Cooked rice

Sliced avocado

INSTRUCTIONS

1. Heat the olive oil in a large pan or skillet over medium heat. Add the sofrito and sauté for 1 to 2 minutes.

2. Add the adobo, sazón, tomato paste, and onion and combine. Continue to cook for 2 to 3 more minutes or until the onion starts to soften. Add a small amount of water if needed to avoid browning.

3. Add the garlic, tomato sauce, water, salt, and pepper and combine. Taste and adjust the seasoning if needed.

4. Add the tofu and, using a spoon, fold in the tomato sauce. Lower the heat to a simmer, cover, and cook for 10 minutes. Check the sauce frequently and feel free to add more water as the sauce thickens to get the right consistency.

5. Once ready, remove from heat and serve with rice and sliced avocado.

Tostones Rellenos
(Tempeh-Stuffed Plantain Cups)

MAKES: 2–4 SERVINGS | PREP TIME: 15 MINUTES | COOKING TIME: 30 MINUTES

To make these flavor-rich *Tostones Rellenos*, plant-based tempeh is the star ingredient. Tostones are a Caribbean staple that can be filled with anything, but most often they're filled with ground beef, shrimp, or chicken. Tempeh is an amazing substitute for ground beef, especially when you season it heavily with aromatic spices. Like tofu, tempeh is made from soybeans, but tempeh has a firmer, chewier texture and a slightly nuttier flavor because it's made from cooked, fermented soybeans. It's a great source of protein, iron, manganese, and phosphorus and it's low in carbs. If you're new to using tempeh, I think it will become your new favorite meat substitute once you see how versatile it can be.

INGREDIENTS

Filling

1 tablespoon olive oil

2 tablespoons Homemade Puerto Rican Sofrito (page 21)

2 tablespoons tomato paste

1 tablespoon Homemade Adobo (page 18)

½ tablespoon Homemade Sazón (page 24)

½ teaspoon dried oregano

1 (8-ounce) block original tempeh cut into 1-inch cubes

½ cup water

2 teaspoons capers

Salt and pepper to taste

Plantain Cups

3 cups olive oil for frying

2 green plantains, peeled and cut into 3-inch rounds

To Serve

Avocado chunks

Pickled red onion

Fresh cilantro

INSTRUCTIONS

1. To make the filling, heat 1 tablespoon olive oil in a pan over medium heat. Add sofrito and tomato paste and sauté for 1 to 2 minutes. Add the adobo, sazón, and oregano and continue to cook for 1 to 2 more minutes.

2. Add the tempeh, water, and capers and combine. Taste and add salt and pepper to your liking.

(Continued)

3. Bring the tempeh mixture to a boil. Once boiling, reduce the heat to a simmer, cover, and let cook for 12 to 15 minutes or until the tempeh has absorbed all the flavors from the sauce. Once ready, shut off the heat and set it aside.

4. To make the plantain cups, heat 3 cups olive oil in a large skillet over high heat. Fry the plantains for 1 to 2 minutes or until lightly browned. Once browned, remove from the oil and place on a plate lined with a paper towel to absorb any excess oil.

5. Use a tostonera or lemon squeezer to stuff plantains and carefully press down on each plantain to form small cups.

6. Place the plantain cups back in the hot oil to fry for about 3 to 4 more minutes or until golden brown. Once ready, remove from the oil and place them back on the plate lined with a paper towel to absorb any excess oil.

7. Stuff each plantain cup with the tempeh filling and top with avocado chunks, pickled red onion, and fresh cilantro.

Yuca con Mojo
(Yuca in Garlic Sauce)

MAKES 2–4 SERVINGS | PREP TIME: 10 MINUTES | COOKING TIME: 30 MINUTES

Yuca is a root veggie that I recommend a lot because it's so healthy and easy to use. It can be boiled, fried, bought frozen or fresh, and it promotes skin health and has a low glycemic index. This popular Cuban dish pairs boiled yuca with the rich, pungent taste of onions and garlic. Usually, you'll find this dish at Christmas or other special holiday meals and even though it's an easy recipe, most families leave it up to the older generation to prepare, out of respect. It's often served with Arroz Congrí (page 69) and pork. Fun fact: Yuca is an ingredient that's been used for thousands of years. In fact, it's the origin of *asaba*, an indigenous *Arahuaco* recipe that uses yuca instead of bread and is served with soup, sancocho, and ceviche. My mom learned to make this from my stepfather's mom, who was Cuban, and I learned to make it from her. Traditionally, it's made with bitter orange marinade, but I subbed in lime juice as a cleaner alternative. This isn't your abuela's recipe, but it's just as delicious!

INGREDIENTS

1 teaspoon salt

1 (24-ounce) bag frozen yuca

1 cup olive oil, divided

2 yellow onions, thinly sliced

3 cloves garlic, minced

2 dried bay leaves

12 black peppercorns

Juice of 2 limes

Salt to taste

To Serve

Arroz Congrí (page 69)

Mushroom Ropa Vieja (page 91)

INSTRUCTIONS

1. Fill a large pot with water and place over medium heat. Add the salt and bring to a boil.

2. Once boiling, add the frozen yuca. Bring the heat down to a simmer, cover, and cook for 15 to 20 minutes or until the yuca is fork tender (but not too tender that it falls apart).

3. Once ready, remove from heat, drain the water, and transfer to a serving dish to cool.

4. While the yuca cools, heat ¼ cup olive oil in a pan or skillet over medium heat.

5. Add the onions and sauté for 2 to 3 minutes or until the onions start to soften. Add the garlic and sauté for 1 to 2 more minutes.

6. To the same pot, add the rest of the olive oil, bay leaves, and black peppercorns and combine. Reduce the heat to simmer and cook for 5 minutes to allow the flavors to come together.

7. Once ready, pour the mixture over the cooked yuca, add lime juice, and combine. Taste and adjust the seasoning if you wish.

8. Serve with Arroz Congrí, Mushroom Ropa Vieja, or both and enjoy!

Postres
(Desserts)

Aquafaba Chocolate Pudding

MAKES: 4–6 SERVINGS | PREP TIME: 15 MINUTES | COOKING TIME: 5 MINUTES

Every time I serve this recipe to someone new, I get the same surprised, delighted, and confused response: "This is made with liquid from a can of chickpeas?" They can't wrap their heads around how Aquafaba (page 7) works and why it doesn't taste like chickpeas. I just smile and tell them, "That's the magic of plant-based cooking." The cream of tartar helps thicken the aquafaba, but don't worry if you can't find it at your grocery store because you can still make this recipe without it. You'll be amazed by how these plant-based ingredients and dairy-free chocolate chips combine for an incredibly rich chocolatey flavor.

INGREDIENTS

1 cup Aquafaba (page 7)

¼ teaspoon cream of tartar

¼ teaspoon salt

1 cup dairy-free chocolate chips, plus more for serving

⅓ cup Homemade Oat Milk (page 145)

To Serve

Fresh raspberries

INSTRUCTIONS

1. Set aside 4 to 6 small ramekins.

2. Add the aquafaba, cream of tartar, and salt to a large mixing bowl. Using an electric hand mixer, mix 5 to 7 minutes or until the mixture forms stiff peaks. Once ready, set it aside.

3. Place a double boiler over medium heat, add in the chocolate chips, and stir occasionally until melted. Once melted, add oat milk and mix to combine, then remove from heat and set aside to cool slightly for 2 to 3 minutes.

4. Pour the chocolate mixture into the bowl with the whipped aquafaba and fold gently to combine.

5. Evenly distribute the mixture into ramekins and place in the refrigerator to set for 2 to 4 hours or overnight.

6. Once set, remove from the refrigerator and top with fresh raspberries and more dairy-free chocolate chips.

Arroz con Leche sin Leche
(Rice Pudding without Milk)

MAKES 4–6 SERVINGS | PREP TIME: 10 MINUTES | COOKING TIME: 35 MINUTES

Unlike the *arroz con dulce* we make in Puerto Rico with coconut milk, this recipe is inspired by Cuban rice pudding, which typically uses cows' milk. All the flavors of Cuban rice pudding are the same, this recipe is just upgraded to be healthier. My mom made this often when I was kid. I have vivid memories of seeing the little plastic cups in the fridge while the pudding chilled, but I actually loved eating it warm and scraping the saucepan, so not a bit of this delicious dessert went to waste. Enjoy this recipe how you like it, hot or cold, and feel free to use almond or oat milk.

INGREDIENTS

3 cups basmati rice, cooked and cooled

4 cups dairy-free milk, unsweetened

½ cup maple syrup

Lime peel, about 2 inches long

1 teaspoon vanilla extract

½ teaspoon ground cinnamon, plus more for serving

⅛ teaspoon sea salt

¼ cup raisins (optional)

INSTRUCTIONS

1. Place a saucepan over medium heat. Add the rice, dairy-free milk, maple syrup, lime peel, vanilla, cinnamon, and salt.

2. Cook uncovered, stirring often, until the rice mixture starts to resemble oatmeal, approximately 20 to 30 minutes.

3. Remove from the heat and carefully remove the lime peel. Add the raisins if using' and combine.

4. Divide the rice pudding into small serving bowls and let cool before placing in the refrigerator to chill for 1 to 2 hours.

5. Serve with more ground cinnamon and enjoy!

Banana Bread

MAKES: 10–12 SERVINGS | PREP TIME: 15 MINUTES | COOKING TIME: 50 MINUTES

The smell of banana bread immediately takes me back to childhood. My mom, the baker in the family, used to enjoy a homemade slice with a cup of coffee, making sure no crumb was left behind. My abuelo also loved any kind of pound cake with a tall glass of milk. I remember sitting on the floor enjoying a half-frozen slice of store-bought pound cake with him in Puerto Rico. This recipe is way better than the prepackaged version my abuelo enjoyed because there are no preservatives. Plus, fresh bananas are a great source of potassium, which can help to lower blood pressure. Walnuts are rich in omega-3 fats and have a high number of antioxidants, so feel free to add a little extra.

INGREDIENTS

5 ripe bananas

¼ cup maple syrup

3 tablespoons chia seeds

½ teaspoon vanilla extract

2 cups oat flour

2½ teaspoons baking powder

1 teaspoon salt

½ teaspoon ground cinnamon

¾ cup walnuts, coarsely chopped

INSTRUCTIONS

1. Preheat the oven to 350°F. Grease a 9 × 5-inch loaf pan with nonstick cooking spray and set aside.

2. In a large mixing bowl, mash the bananas. Add the maple syrup, chia seeds, and vanilla and combine. Cover with a kitchen towel and set aside for 5 minutes.

3. In a separate mixing bowl add the oat flour, baking powder, salt, and ground cinnamon and combine.

4. Pour the banana mixture into the bowl with the dry ingredients and combine.

5. Add in the walnuts and, using a spatula, fold to combine.

6. Pour the banana bread mixture into the greased loaf pan and bake for 45 to 50 minutes or until a toothpick inserted comes out mostly clean.

7. Remove from the oven and let cool before serving.

Barritas de Chocolate
(Chocolate Chip Bars)

MAKES: 12–16 SQUARES | PREP TIME: 15 MINUTES | COOKING TIME: 55 MINUTES

This recipe is a favorite of my daughter's (I've actually never met a kid who *doesn't* love chocolate chips). We spent a lot of our downtime in 2020 making these tasty bars in the kitchen. She's actually so good at making this recipe that when we made a few videos on Instagram sharing the instructions with my community, she took over! In addition to being a great baking activity with kids, this recipe is 100 percent plant-based, while still being sweet and tender—without eggs, milk, or any needless additives. Pure cacao powder is pretty magical because it's packed with flavonoids. These nutrients have been shown to lower blood pressure, improve blood flow to the brain and heart, and even aid in preventing blood clots. It's true that chocolate can be healthy when it's not mixed with sugar, dairy, and additives found in traditional candy bars.

INGREDIENTS

3 ripe bananas

1 teaspoon vanilla extract

¼ cup unsweetened dairy-free milk

1 teaspoon apple cider vinegar

½ cup coconut oil

¾ cup coconut palm sugar

2 cups oat flour

¾ teaspoon baking soda

¼ teaspoon salt

1 cup dairy-free chocolate chips

INSTRUCTIONS

1. Preheat the oven to 350°F. Grease a 9 × 9-inch baking pan with nonstick cooking spray and set aside.

2. In a large mixing bowl, mash the bananas. Add vanilla, dairy-free milk, apple cider vinegar, and coconut oil and combine.

3. In another large mixing bowl, combine the coconut palm sugar, oat flour, baking soda, and salt.

4. Add the dry ingredients to the wet ingredients and combine. Using a spatula, fold in the chocolate chips.

5. Pour the batter into the baking pan and bake for 45 to 55 minutes or until edges are golden and a toothpick inserted comes out mostly clean.

6. Once ready, remove from the oven and allow to cool for 15 minutes before cutting into squares and serving.

Adding apple cider vinegar to your plant-based milk helps curdle the milk, which makes your cakes and cookies super moist. I recommend it to everyone baking with vegan ingredients—it makes a big difference.

Chivato de Calabaza
(Calabaza Custard)

MAKES: 6–8 SERVINGS | PREP TIME: 20 MINUTES | COOKING TIME: 25 MINUTES

This is my Mami Abuelita's famous Christmas dish. She passed this recipe down to family and friends, and it's even on the menu at one of my cousin's restaurants in Puerto Rico. In our family, her cakes and pastries were legendary—we still talk about them. She put so much love into everything she made, and it left an impact on us all. This dairy-free custard tastes like a cross between Flan de Coco (page 133) and pumpkin pie, so you're in for a treat. Naturally healthy and plant-based, the only way I "flipped" this family recipe is by swapping out white sugar for brown sugar. Brown sugar is less processed and, yes, it is still sugar, but it's a healthier alternative! The rich and creamy coconut milk used here has anti-inflammatory and anti-fungal properties and it may support heart health and even reduce stomach ulcers, so you can consider this a dessert that's actually good for you.

INGREDIENTS

9–10 cups (about 4 pounds) calabaza squash, peeled, cubed, and seeds removed

1 cup cornstarch

4 cups full-fat coconut milk

1½ cups coconut palm sugar

2 cinnamon sticks

¾ teaspoon salt

INSTRUCTIONS

1. Set aside a 9-inch pie dish.

2. Add the squash to a large pot and cover with water. Place the pot over medium-high heat and bring to a boil. Once boiling, reduce the heat to medium and let the calabaza squash cook until tender for approximately 12 to 15 minutes. Once tender, drain the calabaza squash, reserving ¾ cup of the water.

3. In a mixing bowl, add the reserved water and cornstarch and whisk to combine. Set it aside.

4. In another large mixing bowl, add the cooked calabaza squash. Using a fork or potato masher, mash and combine the calabaza squash.

5. Place a fine mesh strainer over another mixing bowl. Pour the mashed calabaza squash into the strainer and, using a spoon, press down the calabaza squash into the mixing bowl. Once done, you should have 3 cups of calabaza squash puree.

(Continued)

6. Add the calabaza squash puree back to the large pot over medium heat. Add in the coconut milk, sugar, cinnamon sticks, and salt and combine.

7. Add in the cornstarch mixture and combine.

8. Using a wooden spoon, stir the mixture constantly for 5 to 7 minutes until it starts to thicken.

9. Once ready, carefully remove the cinnamon sticks and pour the mixture into the pie dish. Let cool before placing in the refrigerator to set for 1 to 2 hours.

10. Once set, remove from the refrigerator, cut into slices, serve, and enjoy!

Cranberry and Avena Cookies

MAKES: 12 COOKIES | PREP TIME: 45 MINUTES | COOKING TIME: 12 MINUTES

These cookies will always remind me of Christmas mornings from my childhood. This was my mom's favorite cookie recipe, and she only made them once a year. She added white chocolate chips to hers, but you can customize yours however you like. Using oats as the base of this cookie offers a dose of fiber called beta-glucan which is known to reduce levels of bad cholesterol. Call it a cookie that's actually *good* for your health.

INGREDIENTS

2 cups rolled oats

3 overripe bananas, mashed

½ cup creamy almond butter

½ cup dried cranberries

To Serve

Cashew Condensed Milk (page 11)

Homemade Almond Milk (page 144)

Want to make these safe for someone with a nut allergy? Swap out almond butter for sunflower butter and they'll be just as delicious.

INSTRUCTIONS

1. Preheat the oven to 350°F. Line a large cookie sheet with parchment paper and set it aside.

2. In a large mixing bowl, add all ingredients except the cranberries and combine.

3. Using a spatula, fold in the cranberries.

4. Using a spoon, scoop a small amount of the cookie dough and place it on your lined cookie sheet. Using the same spoon or clean hands, press down on the dough to give it a cookie shape.

5. Bake the cookies in the oven for 10 to 12 minutes or until slightly golden on the edges.

6. Once ready, remove the cookies from the oven and let cool before serving.

7. Enjoy cookies by themselves or with a drizzle of Cashew Condensed Milk and glass of Homemade Almond Milk on the side.

Dulce de Lechosa
(Candied Papaya)

MAKES: 4–6 SERVINGS | PREP TIME: 15 MINUTES | COOKING TIME: 1 HOUR 15 MINUTES

The first time I visited the Dominican Republic with my dad's partner, she took me to local bakeries and sweets shops. It seemed like they candied just about everything: coconut, papaya—I even found candied tomatoes, or *dulce de tomate*, a tomato jam! This recipe is a great way to have a simple dessert. My aunt Tata later told me that my Mami Abuelita candied papaya all the time, so I love this recipe even more. I also love that this is a budget-friendly way to make a family-friendly dessert and use up produce on the edge of going bad. I subbed in brown sugar for a slightly healthier version here but, as you know, sugar should be enjoyed in moderation. I serve this with dairy-free ice cream or just solo. It's really good either way.

INGREDIENTS

1 pound (about 4 cups) semi-ripe papaya, peeled, cut into 1½-inch cubes, and seeds removed

4 tablespoons baking powder

2 cups coconut palm sugar

1 cinnamon stick

1 teaspoon vanilla extract

INSTRUCTIONS

1. To a large mixing bowl, add the papaya and baking powder and cover with water. Cover the bowl with a kitchen towel and let sit for 7 to 8 hours or overnight. This process hardens the papaya and prevents it from falling apart during the cooking process.

2. Once the papaya hardens, remove it from the bowl, rinse the papaya with fresh water, and drain.

3. Place a large pot over low heat. Add the hardened papaya and sugar and cover. Let cook for 30 minutes.

4. After 30 minutes have passed, add the cinnamon stick and vanilla and gently combine. Continue to cook with the pot uncovered for 30 to 45 minutes or until the sugar mixture starts to thicken, then remove from heat and let cool.

5. Once the Dulce de Lechosa has cooled, transfer to a serving bowl and place in the refrigerator to chill for 1 to 2 hours before serving.

Flan de Coco
(Coconut Custard)

MAKES: 4–6 SERVINGS | PREP TIME: 15 MINUTES | COOKING TIME: 15 MINUTES

Flan (or *quesillo* in some Spanish-speaking countries) is a super popular dessert in Latin cuisine. In my family, my mom is the Flan Queen. She is always the one who makes the flan for family holidays and get-togethers. Traditionally, this dessert is made with eggs, sugar, evaporated milk, condensed milk, and vanilla extract. Recently, while she visited me in New York, we decided to "flip" her famous recipe into one that was healthier. After many tries (we made and ate a lot of flan that weekend—poor us!), we got the consistency just right. For this recipe, I replaced eggs with agar-agar powder, a vegetarian gelatin substitute that actually comes from seaweed. I know that may not sound appealing but trust me when I say it doesn't change the taste and it works like a charm to get the perfect plant-based flan. Mom approves of this version, and I know you will, too.

INGREDIENTS

Caramel Sauce

⅓ cup coconut palm sugar

1 tablespoon water

Flan

1 can full-fat coconut milk

¾ teaspoon agar-agar powder (not the flakes)

1 cup unsweetened dairy-free milk

1 teaspoon oat flour

⅓ cup maple syrup

1 teaspoon vanilla extract

⅛ teaspoon salt

INSTRUCTIONS

1. Set aside 4 to 6 small ramekins.

2. To make the caramel, place a small saucepan over medium-low heat. Add the coconut palm sugar and water and stir to combine. Continue to stir until the sugar starts to bubble, about 2 to 3 minutes.

3. Once the sugar starts to bubble, remove from heat and immediately pour into your ramekins. Gently tilt the ramekins to coat the inside with caramel. Set aside and let cool.

(Continued)

4. To make the flan, add the coconut milk and agar-agar powder to a medium saucepan and whisk to combine. Set it aside.

5. To a blender add the dairy-free milk, oat flour, maple syrup, vanilla, and salt and blend until the ingredients are well combined. Pour this mixture into the saucepan with coconut milk and agar-agar powder and whisk to combine.

6. Turn the heat to medium-high and bring the mixture to a simmer for 5 to 7 minutes, stirring occasionally.

7. Carefully pour the flan mixture into the ramekins and let cool 15 minutes before placing in the refrigerator to set for 1 to 2 hours.

8. Once set, remove from the refrigerator and using a small knife, carefully loosen the edges of the flan. Turn the ramekin over onto a plate to release the flan. Serve and enjoy!

Mango Pudding

Many of my clients are afraid of eating fruit in its natural state because they think it's too sugary and it'll lead to weight-gain, but fresh fruits are critical to our diets. They offer important vitamins and minerals and are packed with fiber, which aids digestion, can reduce cholesterol levels, and can even support healthy weight management. In addition to mango (one of my favorite fruits), this dairy-free pudding relies on silken tofu, a plant-based ingredient that's a wonderful substitute for eggs and milk. I use it to make creamy soups, desserts, smoothies, dips, and more. It keeps well in the fridge and works like a dream.

INGREDIENTS

1 (16-ounce) block silken tofu

1½ cups ripe mango cubes

¼ cup maple syrup

2 teaspoons vanilla extract

If you aren't into mango, feel free to swap in other fruits like pineapple or banana.

To Serve

Toasted coconut flakes

INSTRUCTIONS

1. To a blender, add the silken tofu, mango, maple syrup, and vanilla and blend on high until smooth.

2. Pour the mixture into small serving bowls and place them in the refrigerator to set for 2 hours or overnight.

3. Once set, remove from the refrigerator, top with toasted coconut flakes, and enjoy.

Bebidas
(Beverages)

Anti-Inflammatory Smoothie

This tropical fruit smoothie contains two superfoods (a.k.a. a food rich in compounds that benefit your health) that you may already have in your diet: pineapple and papaya. For centuries, papaya has been used to cure burns, inflammation, and pain. It's also packed with powerful antioxidants and nutrients like vitamin C and beta carotene, which not only reduce inflammation but also boost your immunity against viruses, colds, and ear infections. There have been countless studies on the benefits of pineapple, and they all point to one thing: eating pineapple daily can really boost your immunity! Pineapple also contains the enzyme bromelain which can reduce pain from rheumatoid arthritis and osteoarthritis inflammation. This recipe is a perfect example of how plant-based cooking can feel decadent while being full of nutrients.

INGREDIENTS

¾ cup ripe papaya, peeled, cubed, and seeds removed

¾ cup ripe pineapple, peeled and cubed

½ ripe banana, peeled

1 cup dairy-free milk

¼ cup rolled oats

2 tablespoons hemp seeds

1 teaspoon ground cinnamon

INSTRUCTIONS

1. Add all ingredients to a blender and blend on high until smooth and creamy.

2. Evenly distribute into serving glasses and enjoy!

Coquito
(Puerto Rican Eggnog)

MAKES: 15 (4-OUNCE) SERVINGS | PREP TIME: 20 MINUTES | COOKING TIME: 0 MINUTES

Every Puerto Rican family takes pride in their recipe for *coquito*. Just like sofrito, everyone's coquito is a little different—some people add raw eggs and some use star anise. My abuela made hers strong and thick and her handwritten recipe is still circulating in my family. We'd only have it at Christmastime, which made it even more special. Traditionally, it's made with coconut cream, cream of coconut, condensed milk, and evaporated milk with rum and spices. Abuela never drank, so she'd try hers before she added the rum and would ask Abuelo to taste it. He'd give the okay, then add a little more without her noticing! This recipe is inspired by hers but is completely plant-based, using only coconut cream and milk. Fun fact: Many Latin communities have different versions of this drink. In Cuba, there's a similar drink called *crema de vie*, in Mexico, there's *rompope*, and in Venezuela, there's *ponche de creme*.

INGREDIENTS

1½ cups raw cashews, soaked in hot water for 2–4 hours, drained, and rinsed

3 (13½-ounce) cans full-fat coconut milk

1 (13½-ounce) can unsweetened cream of coconut

1 cup maple syrup

1 tablespoon vanilla extract

1 teaspoon ground cinnamon, plus more for serving

¼ teaspoon salt

1½–2 cups white rum (optional)

2–4 cinnamon sticks, divided

2–4 whole vanilla beans, halved lengthwise, divided

INSTRUCTIONS

1. To make coquito, add the soaked cashews, coconut milk, cream of coconut, maple syrup, vanilla extract, ground cinnamon, and salt into a blender and blend on high for 5 to 7 minutes or until smooth.

2. Place a fine mesh strainer over a large mixing bowl and pour the coquito mixture through the strainer to remove any cashew pieces.

3. Add in the rum if using and combine.

4. Place the coquito in the refrigerator for 1 to 2 hours to chill before serving.

5. Once chilled, serve with a sprinkle of ground cinnamon and enjoy!

6. To store coquito, divide cinnamon sticks and vanilla beans between 2–4 glass bottles or mason jars with lids. Evenly distribute the coquito mixture into each glass bottle or jar and seal. Store in the refrigerator for up to a month.

Coquito will thicken and separate when cold so let it sit on the counter for a few minutes and shake before serving.

Homemade Almond Milk

MAKES: 5 CUPS | PREP TIME: 5 MINUTES | COOKING TIME: 0 MINUTES

I know that breaking up with cow's milk can feel . . . impossible. In Latin culture, we are constantly reaching for milk, especially in our daily coffee ritual. I've had clients tell me that their mornings just don't feel right if the coffee doesn't taste right. I get it but, rest assured, I am not here to mess up your morning routine!

INGREDIENTS

1 cup raw almonds, soaked for 8 hours or overnight, drained, and rinsed

5 cups filtered water

¼ teaspoon salt

2 tablespoons maple syrup or 2 pitted dates

1 teaspoon vanilla extract

INSTRUCTIONS

1. To a high-speed blender, add the soaked almonds, water, salt, maple syrup or dates, and vanilla. To make an unsweetened, unflavored almond milk, skip the maple syrup or dates and vanilla extract.

2. Blend on high for 30 seconds.

3. Place a nut milk bag or thin kitchen towel over a large bowl and pour the almond milk into the bag or towel. Strain the liquid into the bowl, squeezing the bag or towel to extract any extra liquid.

4. Transfer the almond milk into an airtight container and store in the refrigerator for up to 4 days.

Separation can occur when the almond milk is in the refrigerator so shake or stir before serving.

Homemade Oat Milk

MAKES: 6 CUPS | PREP TIME: 10 MINUTES | COOKING TIME: 0 MINUTES

Way before oat milk became a trendy dairy-free drink, a version of it was enjoyed in Puerto Rico. When I was growing up, I loved *refresco de avena*, a traditional cold oatmeal drink which literally translates to "oatmeal soda." If you're not a huge fan of almond milk, I recommend trying oat milk—for many folks, it has a more familiar flavor and a better texture. I love making oat milk at home because it's budget-friendly and preservative- and additive-free. Experiment using homemade oat milk in everything from coffee to smoothies. You can even enjoy a tall glass of it, like you might enjoy a *refresco de avena*. You know, for old times' sake.

INGREDIENTS

1 cup whole rolled oats

6 cups filtered water

2 tablespoons maple syrup or 2 pitted dates

1 teaspoon vanilla extract

¼ teaspoon sea salt

INSTRUCTIONS

1. Add the oats, water, maple syrup or dates, vanilla, and salt into a high-speed blender and blend on high for 30 seconds. To make an unsweetened, unflavored oat milk, skip the maple syrup or dates and vanilla extract.

2. Place a fine mesh strainer over a large bowl and strain the oat milk without pushing any of the oats through the strainer.

3. Transfer the oat milk to an airtight container and store in the refrigerator for up to 4 days.

Separation can occur when the oat milk is in the refrigerator so simply shake or

Kombucha Mocktail

MAKES: 2–4 SERVINGS | PREP TIME: 10 MINUTES | COOKING TIME: 0 MINUTES

Kombucha is, in a word, magical. If you've never had it before, I think you'll love it, especially if you are a fan of carbonated drinks. Kombucha is a fermented, sweet, fizzy tea drink that also happens to be great for you. It helps digestion, detoxifies your body, and can boost your energy. I love to make a kombucha "mocktail," a cocktail without the alcohol, on warm summer days. I joke that it's the perfect "in between" drink when you aren't sure if it's too early for a real cocktail or not. Jokes aside, this is a delightful drink I recommend if you are limiting your alcohol or soda intake and still want something refreshing to enjoy at your next party.

INGREDIENTS

1½ cups kombucha of choice (apple, ginger, or original flavor)

½ cup apple juice

2 ounces fresh lime juice

To Serve

Ice

Sparkling water

Lime wedges

Fresh fruit, chopped (optional)

INSTRUCTIONS

1. In a pitcher, add kombucha, apple juice, and lime juice and stir to combine.

2. To serve, add ice into a few glasses, fill each glass ¾ of the way with kombucha mix, top with sparkling water, and stir to combine. Garnish with lime wedges and fruit. Enjoy!

Piña Colada

MAKES: 2–4 SERVINGS | PREP TIME: 10 MINUTES | COOKING TIME: 0 MINUTES

If you love piña coladas (who doesn't?), you should know that this beloved drink of coconut cream, pineapple juice, white rum, and ice was invented in San Juan, Puerto Rico. Naturally, I had to include a piña colada recipe in this book—but flipped into an upgraded version, of course. This recipe is inspired by my dad, who doesn't drink alcohol. When we're out, he always orders a virgin piña colada. Now, whenever I order one, I always think of him. Traditionally, this drink often comes with many processed ingredients. This recipe is alcohol-free and uses natural sweeteners instead. I think you'll taste the difference. Cheers!

INGREDIENTS

1 (13½-ounce) can light coconut milk

1 teaspoon vanilla extract

3 cups frozen pineapple

2 tablespoons maple syrup or more for a sweeter taste

To Serve (optional)

Fresh pineapple slices

Lime wedges

INSTRUCTIONS

1. Add the coconut milk, vanilla, frozen pineapple, and maple syrup to a blender and blend on high until smooth.

2. Pour into glasses and garnish with fresh pineapple slices and lime wedges. Enjoy!

Sangria

Sangria is a drink that has stood the test of time. It actually dates back to 200 BC! Ancient Romans enjoyed drinking red wines from Spain and named their wines and wine-based punches sangria. Later, sangria became a popular drink all over Europe, specifically sangrias made with French Bordeaux wines as the base. What I love about sangria is that it's so easy to improvise. You can use whatever wine you have on hand and whatever fruits. Lemons, oranges, and strawberries work, but I love adding apples and pears because they have so much fiber (yes, even fruits in your drinks count as adding nutrition to your day!).

INGREDIENTS

1 bottle (750 milliliters) red wine of choice

1 lemon

1 lime

1 orange

1 apple, core removed and cut into small cubes

1 pear, core removed and cut into small cubes

½ cup maple syrup

To Serve

Ice cubes

Sparkling water

INSTRUCTIONS

1. Pour the wine into a pitcher. Squeeze in the juice of the lemon, lime, and orange and drop the rinds into the pitcher.

2. Add in the apple, pear, and maple syrup and stir to combine.

3. Place the pitcher in the refrigerator to chill for 1 to 2 hours.

4. To serve, add a few ice cubes to a wine glass, fill the glass ¾ of the way with Sangria, and top with sparkling water.

Upgraded Margarita

MAKES: 1 SERVING | PREP TIME: 10 MINUTES | COOKING TIME: 0 MINUTES

Enjoying an occasional margarita is truly a treat. Alcohol is never going to be a "healthy" choice because it's naturally inflammatory, and sugary drinks with processed ingredients are even worse, but if you do decide to have a drink, choose this "flipped" margarita (and drink responsibly). You can make cocktails like this one cleaner with a few ingredient upgrades. For example, this recipe uses maple syrup instead of simple syrup. Since maple syrup is high in antioxidants and other nutrients like riboflavin, zinc, and calcium, I use it as much as possible when I want to sweeten a drink or even a dessert. Next time you're hosting, you can multiply this recipe to make a batch of naturally sweet margarita; your guests will never know about your syrup swap.

INGREDIENTS

Lime wedge, to rim the glass

Salt

3 tablespoons fresh lime juice

1½ tablespoons orange juice

2 ounces silver tequila

1 teaspoon maple syrup

To Serve

Lime wheel (optional)

Orange wheel (optional)

INSTRUCTIONS

1. Rim the top edge of a glass with the lime wedge. Pour a thin layer of salt onto a small plate, then dip the glass into the salt. Fill the glass with ice and set it aside.

2. To a cocktail shaker, add lime juice, orange juice, tequila, maple syrup, and ice. Close the cocktail shaker and shake for 30 seconds.

3. Pour the mixture into the rimmed glass, garnish with a lime and orange wheel if using, and enjoy!

About the Author

Karla Salinari is a certified holistic health coach who specializes in the plant-based lifestyle. Karla works with clients to meet their health goals through a highly individualized approach that yields transformative, long-lasting habits.

Her popular Instagram account @TheLatinaHealthCoach inspires others to reconnect with their favorite cultural dishes in a healthier way. The enthusiastic response from her followers led to the creation of this book.

Karla earned a certification in holistic nutrition from the Institute of Integrative Nutrition in New York City and she's a frequent TV guest expert on Telemundo and NBC. Born in California and raised in Miami and Puerto Rico, she now lives in Brooklyn, New York, with her husband and daughter.

Acknowledgments

It's true that food truly brings people together, and writing a cookbook is proof. Though it's deeply personal to memorialize your family recipes, I had a community of people lending their talents and support to this project every step of the way. Without them, this book wouldn't exist, so I'd like to express my deep gratitude to the following people, in no particular order:

To my daughter, **Carolina**, for motivating me to know better and do better every single day.

My husband **Joe**, who encouraged me to start using my stove back when we were dating. Without you, I never would've taken my shoes out of the oven (a storage hack every young woman in Manhattan knows). You sparked my curiosity about cooking, and I am eternally grateful for your endless support and open-mindedness about plant-based eating.

My **mom**, for always creating such memorable meals with so much attention and love. Your meticulous approach to baking and cooking gave me an appreciation for how food is prepared. Your wisdom is with me every time I step into the kitchen.

My **dad**, for planting the seed about vegetarianism at a very early age. You showed me that food can be healing, and throughout my journey, I've deepened my spiritual relationship to food.

Tata, who gave me a "behind-the-scenes" look at vegetarian cooking and entrepreneurship when I was a kid. Thank you for letting me peel potatoes in your restaurant (even if I over-peeled them!) and for preserving so many of these family recipes.

Mami Abuelita, the home chef of my family whose composition notebook of short-hand recipes inspired this book—your legacy lives on. Thank you for feeding our family with meals we still talk about and make ourselves. It's a gift that brings us together again and again and now, I hope it will bring other families together.

To my **grandparents**, my brother **Manny**, my **cousins**, **aunts**, and **uncles** for all the memories we made around the table.

To my **friends**, thank you for your decades-long support and for cheering me on while I was juggling mom life, a full-time job, and this book. You saw me through the proposal process to the final product and I am forever grateful.

The **talented team of women** who were with me throughout the entire creative process. Thank you to food photographer Zuleika Acosta for photographing everything so beautifully, to food stylist Sophia Loch for making this food look absolutely delicious, to copywriter Sara Graham for helping me find the right words, and of course Faride Mereb, my "Book Doula" who literally brought this book to life. I can't thank you enough for managing dates, wrangling people, offering edits, and your amazing eye for art direction.

To **Miss Lauren** for stepping in at a moment's notice to be our lovely hand model.

A big thank you to the **Latina Health Coach Instagram and Facebook community** and all of the women who have trusted me to guide them in their plant-based health journey. I feel so lucky to have such an amazing community. Thank you also to the **health coaches at Institute for Integrated Nutrition (IIN)** in New York City who taught me so much.

My agent **Joelle Delbourgo** who had faith in me and this book from the very beginning.

To **everyone at Skyhorse Publishing** for taking a chance on me and believing this book needed to be in the world.

Thank you also to Steve Lachenauer, Gretchen Mendez, everyone who tasted and tried a recipe, Joanne Spataro, and every single one of my readers during this process.

Conversion Charts

METRIC AND IMPERIAL CONVERSIONS

(These conversions are rounded for convenience)

Ingredient	Cups/Tablespoons/Teaspoons	Ounces	Grams/Milliliters
Cornstarch	1 tablespoon	0.3 ounce	8 grams
Dairy-free butter	1 cup/ 16 tablespoons/ 2 sticks	8 ounces	230 grams
Dairy-free cheese, shredded	1 cup	4 ounces	110 grams
Flour, chickpea	1 cup	3.5 ounces	100 grams
Flour, oat	1 cup	3.17 ounces	90 grams
Fruits or veggies, chopped	1 cup	5 to 7 ounces	145 to 200 grams
Fruits or veggies, pureed	1 cup	8.5 ounces	245 grams
Honey or maple syrup	1 tablespoon	0.75 ounce	20 grams
Liquids: dairy-free milk, water, or juice	1 cup	8 fluid ounces	240 milliliters
Oats	1 cup	5.5 ounces	150 grams
Salt	1 teaspoon	0.2 ounce	6 grams
Spices (ground)	1 teaspoon	0.2 ounce	5 milliliters
Sugar, brown, firmly packed	1 cup	7 ounces	200 grams
Vanilla extract	1 teaspoon	0.2 ounce	4 grams

OVEN TEMPERATURES

Fahrenheit	Celsius	Gas Mark
225°	110°	¼
250°	120°	½
275°	140°	1
300°	150°	2
325°	160°	3
350°	180°	4
375°	190°	5
400°	200°	6
425°	220°	7
450°	230°	8

Recipe Index

Ingredient Index

Notes

Notes

Notes

Notes

Notes